AN R COMPANION FOR *THE FUNDAMENTALS OF SOCIAL RESEARCH*

An R Companion for The Fundamentals of Social Research offers students the opportunity to delve into the world of R using real data sets and statistical analysis techniques directly from Paul M. Kellstedt, Guy D. Whitten, and Steven A. Tuch's new textbook. Workbook sections parallel chapters in the main text, giving students a chance to apply the lessons and techniques learned in each chapter in a statistical software setting. Detailed chapters teach students to reproduce results presented in the textbook, allowing them to become comfortable performing statistical analyses for evaluating causal claims through repeated practice. Step-by-step instructions for using R are provided, along with command lines and screenshots to demonstrate proper use of the software. Instructions for producing the figures and tables in the main text are integrated throughout the workbook. End-of-chapter exercises encourage students to formulate and evaluate their own hypotheses.

Paul M. Kellstedt is a professor of political science at Texas A&M University.

Guy D. Whitten is a professor of political science and Director of the European Union Center at Texas A&M University.

Steven A. Tuch is a professor of sociology and public policy and public administration at George Washington University.

AN R COMPANION FOR

The Fundamentals of Social Research

Paul M. Kellstedt

Texas A&M University

Guy D. Whitten

Texas A&M University

Steven A. Tuch

George Washington University

CAMBRIDGE
UNIVERSITY PRESS

CAMBRIDGE
UNIVERSITY PRESS

University Printing House, Cambridge CB2 8BS, United Kingdom

One Liberty Plaza, 20th Floor, New York, NY 10006, USA

477 Williamstown Road, Port Melbourne, VIC 3207, Australia

314–321, 3rd Floor, Plot 3, Splendor Forum, Jasola District Centre,
New Delhi – 110025, India

103 Penang Road, #05–06/07, Visioncrest Commercial, Singapore 238467

Cambridge University Press is part of the University of Cambridge.

It furthers the University's mission by disseminating knowledge in the pursuit of
education, learning, and research at the highest international levels of excellence.

www.cambridge.org
Information on this title: www.cambridge.org/highereducation/isbn/9781009248914
DOI: 10.1017/9781009248938

© Paul M. Kellstedt, Guy D. Whitten, and Steven A. Tuch 2023

First published 2023

A catalogue record for this publication is available from the British Library.

ISBN 978-1-009-24891-4 Paperback

Brief Contents

Contents

Figures

Preface

This software companion book represents an effort to provide both extra exercises, as well as hands-on material for how to put the techniques that we discuss in *The Fundamentals of Social Research* into action. It is one of three workbooks, each written to help students to work with the materials covered in *The Fundamentals of Social Research* using a particular piece of statistical software.

This workbook focuses on using the program R from another program, RStudio. (The other companion books are designed to work with SPSS and Stata.) Our expectation is that the typical user of this book will be using a relatively recent version of R and RStudio. We have written this workbook on a computer running the Windows operating system, but, with a very small number of exceptions, it should work identically for users of different operating systems. An online appendix available at www.cambridge.org/fsr provides users with instructions for installing R and RStudio and other technical issues relating to the use of these programs for the purposes covered in this book.

The chapter structure of this workbook mirrors the chapter structure of *The Fundamentals of Social Research*. We have written with the expectation that students will read the chapters of this companion after they have read the chapters of the book.

We owe a special thank you to Andrea Junqueira for her help with the writing of R code for this workbook.

We continue to update both the general and instructor-only sections of the webpage for our book (www.cambridge.org/fsr). As before, the general section contains data sets available in formats compatible with SPSS, Stata, and R. The instructor-only section contains several additional resources, including PowerPoint and TeX/Beamer slides for each chapter, a test-bank, and answer keys for the exercises.

1 The Scientific Study of Society

1.1 OVERVIEW

In this chapter we introduce you to some of the important building blocks of a scientific approach to studying the social world. As you can already tell from reading the first chapter of *The Fundamentals of Social Research* – which we will refer to as "*FSR*" or the "main text" from here on – data are an important part of what we do both to explore the world and to test hypotheses based on causal theories. An important part of working with data is learning how to use a statistical software package. In the sections that follow, we introduce you to the R program and some basics that you will need to get up and running. In doing this, we also introduce some general principles of good computing practices for effectively working with data.

1.2 "A WORKBOOK? WHY IS THERE A WORKBOOK?"

You might be asking yourself this question, and it's perfectly fair to do so. Allow us to try to explain how this workbook fits in with the main *FSR* text.

As you will see in the weeks and months to follow in your class, the main textbook will teach you about the use of statistics in the social sciences, mostly by using equations and examples. So yes, in some ways, it will feel rather math-y. (And we think that's cool, though we realize that it's not everyone's cup of tea.) One of the ways that people learn about the practice of statistics is to use computer software to calculate statistics directly. To that end, many instructors want students to learn to use a particular computer software package so they can begin to conduct statistical analyses themselves.[1] We have discovered through years of teaching that this transition between equations in a book and software output on a computer screen is a very difficult one. The goal of this software companion book is to make this connection stronger, even seamless.

If we are successful, this book will do two things. First, it will teach the nuts and bolts about how to use R. Though many (perhaps most) students today are quite computer-literate, we believe that having a reference guide for students to learn the techniques, or for them to teach themselves out of class time, will be helpful. Second, and more importantly, this software guide will provide explicit hand-holding to you as you learn to connect the key principles from the main text to the practical issues of producing and interpreting statistical results.

Each chapter of this software guide works in parallel with that of the main *FSR* text. So when you learn the equations of two-variable regression analysis in Chapter 10 of the main text, you will learn the details about using R to estimate two-variable regression models in Chapter 10 of this companion book. And so on. In the end, we hope that the very important (but perhaps rather abstract) equations in the text become more meaningful to you as you learn to estimate the statistics yourself, and then to learn to interpret them meaningfully and clearly. Those three things – formulae, software, and interpretation – together provide a very solid foundation and basic understanding of social science.

1.2.1   Reading Commands in This Workbook

Throughout this workbook, when we present R commands in their text versions, we will write out commands in typewriter type to help distinguish actual R commands from our instructional text. For instance,

```
summary(Reg1)
```

is an example of a command that we would issue if we had previously estimated a regression model which we called "Reg1" and we wanted R to produce a summary table of the results. Occasionally, we will also use italics within a command line to indicate a place in the code where something needs to be placed, but where the exact text of the command depends on what the user is trying to accomplish with that command. So, for instance, in the next chapter where we demonstrate one way to install a new package

---

[1] This particular software companion book teaches students to use R, but we have also produced parallel books for instructors who wish to have their students learn SPSS or Stata.

using the "`install.packages`" command, we will write the following code:

```
install.packages("PackageName")
```

where "*PackageName*" is not what one should enter into the command line (there is not a package named "*PackageName*"), but rather a placeholder written in italics to indicate that one should enter in that part of the code the name of the package that one wants to install.

1.3 GETTING STARTED WITH R AND RSTUDIO

To get started with R and RStudio, we recommend that you set yourself up in front of a computer that has both of the programs installed with a copy of *FSR* close by. You should also have the set of computer files that accompany this text (which you can download from the text's website, www.cambridge.org/fsr) in a directory on the computer on which you are working. You will get the most out of this workbook by working in RStudio as you read this workbook.[2]

The instructions in this book can help you learn R whether you use a Windows-based PC or a Mac. Once the program is launched, R in RStudio works identically, no matter which platform you use. Mac users should be aware, though, that our screenshots will come from a Windows-based PC. Some of those screenshots that involve finding and opening files on your computer, therefore, will look somewhat unfamiliar to Mac users, but we assume that Mac users are at least somewhat used to this. Overall, the differences between running R in RStudio on Windows compared to a Mac are minimal. That said, we have created a help guide on the differences between working with R in RStudio on a Windows-based PC and a Mac operating system, which can be found online at www.cambridge .org/fsr.

Finally, we wrote this book while using versions 4.0.3 of R and the free version of RStudio 1.3.1093. Particularly for the statistical fundamentals you will learn in this book, the differences between versions are not severe. But, since both programs are available for free and easy to install, we recommend that you use the versions that we are using or a newer version of these programs.

---

[2] As we mention in the preface to this book, an online appendix available at www .cambridge.org/fsr provides users with instructions for installing R and RStudio and other technical issues relating to the use of these programs for the purposes covered in this book.

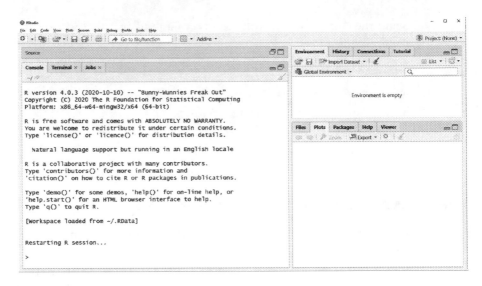

Figure 1.1 RStudio initial launch

1.3.1   Launching RStudio

When you are sitting in front of a computer on which RStudio and R have been properly installed, you can launch the program by double-clicking on the RStudio icon or by finding the RStudio program on your start menu. At this point, you should see one large window like that in Figure 1.1. Within this main window, you will see three other windows labeled "Console" (on the left side), "Environment" (on the top right side), and "Plots" (on the bottom right side). If you are seeing all of this, you are ready to go.

1.3.2   Getting R to Do Things

In almost any mainstream statistical program today, there are multiple ways to accomplish the same tasks. In R in RStudio, the two most common ways to execute commands are by typing them in the console next to the blue > symbol or by typing them into a script in the editor, selecting the command, and hitting the "run" button. The choice of which of these options to use is a matter of personal comfort. But, as we discuss below, no matter which way you choose to get R to do things, you need to keep track of what you are doing. We now discuss the two ways to get R to do things by showing an example of opening a data set. We recommend that you try them both, but especially the example of using a script in the second subsection below.

Typing Commands in the Console Window

You can type commands directly into the console window that you see on the left side of RStudio when you launch the program. These commands are typed in one at a time, and are executed by the program when you hit the "Enter" button on your keyboard.

So, if we want to load the data set "African American Home Ownership 1985-2014" which is an R-format data set (with the ".RData" suffix), you would type the following command into the "Console" window and hit the "Enter" key on your computer:

```
load("C:/MyFSRrFiles/African American Home Ownership
1985-2014.RData")
```

To check whether you have done this correctly, you can click the tab labeled "Environment" in the upper-right window of RStudio. If you have successfully loaded the data, your RStudio will look like Figure 1.2, where we now see the name of the data set that we were attempting to load and a brief summary of how many observations and variables are in the data set.[3]

Using a Script File

A second way to issue commands in RStudio is to use a script file. While this method of working will seem a little bit clumsy at first, it is our preferred method of working in RStudio for reasons that we will explain below. To start work with a new script file, you need to left-click on the "file" tab in the very upper-left corner of the program, and then from the menu that drops down select "New File," followed by "R Script." Once you have successfully done this, your RStudio should look like Figure 1.3. We will eventually cover a lot of different things that one can do with a script file,

---

[3] The location of files is often a stumbling block for beginning users of a statistical software package. To keep things simple, we recommend that you create a folder on your computer's C drive named "MyFSRrFiles" and put all of the files that you have downloaded from www.cambridge.org/fsr into that folder. If you are unable to do this, then on a computer using a Windows operating system you can find the exact name of the location of a file by right-clicking on that file, left-clicking "Properties," and then looking at the entry to the right of "Location." This filepath, or location, can be selected, copied, and pasted directly into your console window (or script) to ensure that it is exactly right. But, it is important to note that the slashes to tell R the location of a file are forward slashes instead of the usual Windows convention of using backslashes. As discussed earlier, a help guide on the differences between working on a Windows-based PC and a Mac operating system can be found online at www.cambridge.org/fsr.

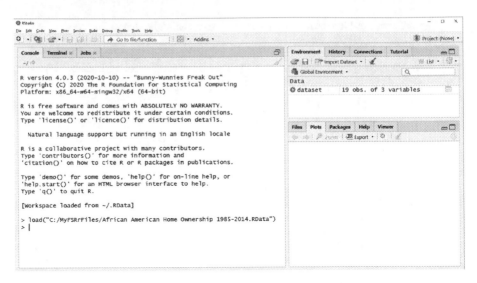

Figure 1.2 Data set successfully loaded into R

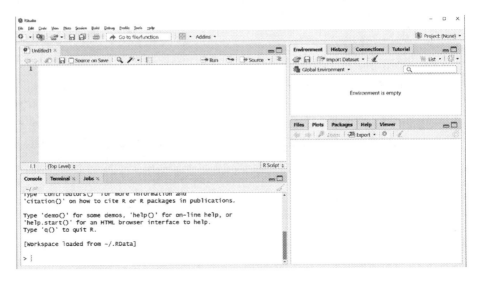

Figure 1.3 Script editor window open

but, for now, all that we want you to do is to type the following command into the new script file:

```
load("C:/MyFSRrFiles/African American Home Ownership
1985-2014.RData")
```

Once you have typed this command into the script-file editor, you next select the entire line – you can do this by left-clicking at the beginning of the line and then moving to the end and releasing the left mouse button – and then click on the "Run" button at the right side of the top of the script-file editor window that has a green arrow pointing from a box toward the word

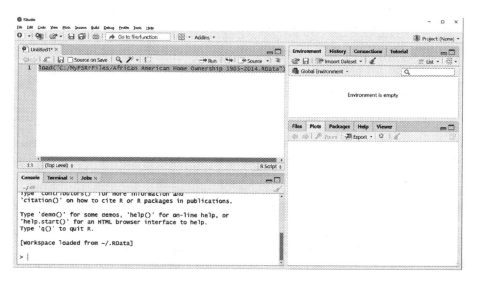

Figure 1.4 Preparing to execute a command from the script-file editor

"Run." Clicking on this button tells the program to execute the selected line or lines of code.[4] In Figure 1.4, we show what this will look like right before you click on "Run." Once you have done this correctly, your RStudio should look like Figure 1.5. And, to further check that you did this correctly, when you left-click on the "Environment" tab in the upper-right corner window, you should see the same contents in that window as what you see in Figure 1.5.

1.3.3 Initially Examining Data in R

Now that we have shown you two different ways to get a data set into R, we want you to take a look at the data that you have loaded into the program.[5] These data are from the 1985–2014 General Social Surveys (GSSs), a data set that you will become quite familiar with in your course, because we make extensive use of it both in this workbook as well as in the main text. The particular survey question that we examine in this illustration asks respondents whether they own or rent the dwelling in which they currently live. To get an initial look at these data, click on the word "dataset" in the "Environment" window in the upper-right corner of RStudio. Once you

---

[4] This also works for selecting multiple lines of code, as we do later in this file. It is worth noting two additional things. First, you don't have to select the entire line of code to submit it as long as your cursor is located somewhere in the line that you wish to run. And second, instead of clicking the "Run" button, you can run code by hitting the "Control" and "Enter" keys at the same time (Ctrl + Enter).

[5] We discuss how to manually enter your own data into an R file in an online appendix, available at www.cambridge.org/fsr.

Figure 1.5 RStudio after having successfully run a command from the script-file editor

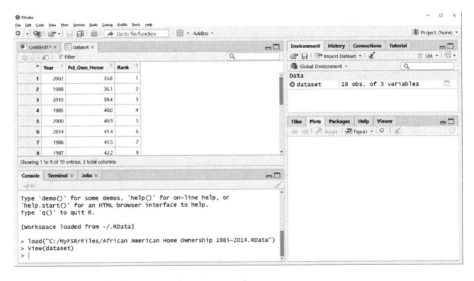

Figure 1.6 Initially examining data in RStudio

have done this, your RStudio should look like Figure 1.6. Each column in this spreadsheet contains values for a particular variable and each row contains data from a single survey year.

In Figure 1.6, you will see data in three columns, labeled from left to right as "Year," "Pct_Own_Home," and "Rank." Those labels correspond to the names of the three variables in our data set. Down the rows you will see the cases of the three variables. For example, in row 10 of the data window, which is the tenth case in the data set, we see the following values for the three variables. "Year" takes on the value of 1993, "Pct_Own_Home" has the value of 43.90, and "Rank" has the value 10.00. These variable names make clear what each variable represents and what the corresponding values mean.

You can use the bars at the right and at the bottom of the data set to scroll through it. As you already know, this data set has only three variables, so all three columns fit in the upper-left window of RStudio; but with data sets with more variables, you will need to use the bars to scroll to the right to see any other variables. Similarly, you can use the bar at the right of the screen to scroll down to see all of the cases in your data set. For now, when you use the bar on the right to scroll down, you'll notice that the last of our cases has a value for "Year" of 1990 and a value for "Pct_Own_Home" of 54.90. You can also see that the data set has a total of nineteen cases.

1.3.4 Adding Notes to Script Files and Saving Them

The main advantage of script files is that they can be saved. This allows users to go back later and see exactly what they did. Once you start writing longer script files, it is a good idea to make notes in them about what you are doing and why you are doing it. We can make notes in script files by starting the line on which we want to write notes with a hash symbol (#). When you ask RStudio to run a command line that starts with #, R reads that symbol as "ignore everything to the right of this symbol on this line of code" and, appropriately, does nothing. This is colloquially known as "commenting out a line" of code. This is helpful when we want to submit an entire script file to R at one time but still have notes about what we did. The programs that are available on the webpage for our book (www .cambridge.org/fsr) contain commented-out lines that explain what is going on in them.[6]

In Figure 1.7 we have clicked back on the R script that we created to load our data set. Notice that we have added a comment at the top of the script file, preceded by a #, that tells us what this script is. It is normally a good idea to add additional lines of comments that identify the person who wrote the code and the date on which the script file was created.

---

[6] You may also want to use the # symbol to add notes to part of a line of code. In this case, you would just put whatever note you want to add to the right of the # and anything that you don't wish to comment out to the left of the #.

Figure 1.7 Script with comment line saved

1.4   EXERCISES

1. Go through all of the steps described above. Once you have the "Data View" open (so that your computer looks like Figure 1.6), do the following:

(a) Look at the values in the column labeled "Pct_Own_Home." This is our measure of homeownership. Do the following:

   i. Identify the year with the highest value for this variable.

   ii. Identify the year with the lowest value for this variable.

   iii. What does it mean if this variable goes up by one?

(b) Look at the values in the column labeled "Rank." This is our measure of the rank, from lowest to highest, of the proportion of African American homeownership in the years from 1985 to 2014. Now do the following:

   i. Identify the year with the highest value for this variable.

   ii. Identify the year with the lowest value for this variable.

   iii. What does it mean if this variable goes up by one?

2 The Art of Theory Building

2.1 OVERVIEW

One of our emphases in FSR is on producing new causal theories, and then evaluating whether or not those theories are supported by evidence. In this chapter, we describe how to explore sources of variation – both across space, and across time – to get you started thinking about new explanations for interesting phenomena. We also help you explore how new theories can be built upon the existing work in the literature. Before we can explore data, however, we need to do a little bit of work in R to get access to the commands that we will use.

2.2 R PACKAGES

One of the great things about R is that the user community is constantly producing new tools that are available for everyone using the program. These new tools are made available in the form of programming modules called "packages." Once you have R and RStudio installed on your computer, you can add additional packages in at least the following three different ways:

1. By left-clicking on the "Tools" located in the upper-left corner of RStudio, and then selecting "Install Packages." This will launch a pop-up window in which you should type the name of the package that you wish to install and then left-click the "Install" button.
2. By left-clicking on the word "Packages" at the top of the bottom-right window. You then see a list of packages that you already have installed on your computer. From there, you can select the search window (next to a magnifying glass) to allow you to search for a particular package and install it.
3. By running the following command (either from the console or a script file): `install.packages("PackageName")`.

Figure 2.1 Packages installed by script

At the time that we are preparing this guide, there are over 10,000 packages available for R. In order to do all of the things that we discuss in this book, you will need the following packages:

- tidyverse
- gmodels
- labelled
- psych
- lm.beta
- car

In Figure 2.1 we can see a script written to install all of these packages. Note that, depending on the speed of your computer and your connection to the Internet, this script might take some time to run. You can tell that it has finished when you see a blue > symbol at the bottom of the console window like what we see in Figure 2.1.

It is worth noting that every time you start an RStudio session, you will need to tell the program which packages you wish to use. This is done with a "library" command. For instance,

```
library(tidyverse)
```

tells R to load the package "tidyverse," which is a package that provides access to a large set of commands that all follow a similar structure.[1]

---

[1] Tidyverse is actually a collection of packages. For more information on this, visit www .tidyverse.org.

2.3 EXAMINING VARIATION ACROSS TIME AND ACROSS SPACE

As we discuss in Section 2.3 of *FSR*, one way to develop ideas about causal theories is to identify interesting variation. In that section, we discuss examining two types of variation, cross-sectional and time-series variation. In this section, we show you how to create figures like the ones presented in Section 2.3 of *FSR*. Although there are many different types of graphs that can be used to examine variation in variables, we recommend a bar graph for cross-sectional variation and a connected plot for time-series variation.

As you will see from these examples, R's graph commands can often be quite long because of all of the options that we typically like to include. We therefore recommend that you start with the main command and then add the options until you get a figure that looks right to you. For the example of the bar graph, we go through steps along these lines in some detail. In later presentations, we will show the final product.

2.3.1 Producing a Bar Graph for Examining Cross-Sectional Variation

A useful way to get a sense of the variation for a cross-sectional variable is to produce a bar graph in which you display the values of that variable across spatial units. In the example that we display in Figure 2.2 of *FSR*, we have a bar graph of Gini coefficients in 2013 for twenty-three randomly selected nations. Building on what we have learned about R so far, we will now show you how to produce a figure like this. First, we need to load the tidyverse package:

```
library(tidyverse)
```

The second step is to load in the data:

```
load("C:/MyFSRrFiles/Gini_coefficients_2013.RData")
```

which will load the appropriate data set into R. Once you have this data set properly loaded into R, you will want to issue a command to produce a bar graph of the variable GiniCoeff for each spatial unit. In this case, the spatial unit is Country. A command for producing such a bar graph is:

```
ggplot(data=Gini_coefficients_2013, aes(x=Country,
y=GiniCoeff)) +
geom_bar(stat="identity") +
theme_bw()
```

where "ggplot" tells R that we want to use the ggplot package. The next part of the command, "Gini_coefficients_2013," is the name of the data set that we wish to use. The "aes" is short for "aesthetic mappings,"

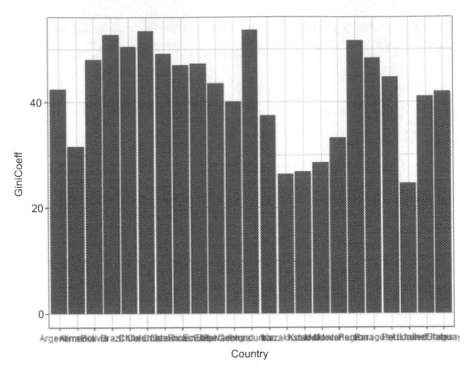

Figure 2.2 Initial bar graph of Gini coefficients

which is a way of communicating to the program which variables are going to play what roles in the figure that we wish to create. In this case, since we are producing a bar graph, we use "y" to tell R the name of the variable for which we wish to display the values in bars, GiniCoeff, and "x" to tell R the name of the variable for which the bars will reflect spatial units or cases, Country. The "+" is entered into the script as a part of the ggplot syntax which tells R that we are going to add some new features to the plot.[2] Continuing on the second line, geom_bar tells R that we want to produce a bar graph, stat="identity" tells R that we want to use the value of y to determine the height of the bars, and theme_bw() tells R that we want to use a simple graph theme with black bars on a white background with grid lines in the background. When you run this command, the resulting graph will appear in the lower-right quadrant of RStudio, and that graph is displayed in Figure 2.2.

One problem that we can see right away in Figure 2.2 is that it is all but impossible to read the names of the countries along the bottom of the horizontal axis. We can fix this by adding to our code as follows:

```
ggplot(data=Gini_coefficients_2013, aes(x=Country,
y=GiniCoeff)) +
geom_bar(stat="identity") +
theme_bw() +
```

---

[2] Unlike the default settings for other statistical programs, in R you do not need to add special characters to tell the program that a command extends over multiple lines.

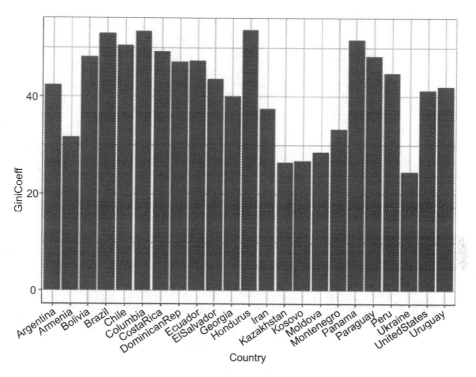

Figure 2.3 Initial bar graph of Gini coefficients with angled country names

```
theme(axis.text.x = element_text(angle=30, hjust=1,
vjust=1))
```

where the additional line of code tells R that we want to adjust the theme further by changing the horizontal axis text, `axis.text.x`, such that each element is now at a 30 degree angle, `(angle=30, hjust=1, vjust=1)`. The resulting graph is displayed in Figure 2.3.

Compare Figure 2.3 here with Figure 2.2 in *FSR*. What is the difference between these two figures? The answer is that in Figure 2.2 in *FSR* the values of the Gini coefficients have been sorted from smallest to largest, and the country names are labeled vertically. When displaying data in graphs, it is important that you do so in a fashion that allows you and your readers to most easily make the assessments that they want to make. In this case, since we are trying to think about what makes a country have a higher or lower Gini coefficient, we want to be able to see which countries have higher or lower values. Try comparing the value of the Gini coefficient between Argentina and El Salvador in the graph that we just made, Figure 2.3. Not an easy thing to do! It's a lot easier using Figure 2.2 from *FSR* because the cases have been *sorted*. You might have also noticed that the label on the vertical axis in Figure 2.2 from *FSR* is more informative. We can make these two adjustments by writing the command as

```
ggplot(data=Gini_coefficients_2013,
aes(x=reorder(Country, GiniCoeff), y=GiniCoeff)) +
geom_bar(stat="identity") +
```

```
theme_bw() +
theme(axis.text.x = element_text(angle=30, hjust=1,
vjust=1)) +
ylab("2013 Gini Coefficients") +
xlab("")
```

where x=reorder(Country, GiniCoeff) tells R to sort the bars based on the value of the variable GiniCoeff, ylab("2013 Gini Coefficients") produces a more informative label on the vertical axis, and xlab("") removes the unnecessary horizontal axis label. The figure that this code produces is not identical to Figure 2.2 in *FSR* because that figure was created in SPSS, but it is very similar.

All of the commands for this example are contained in a script file called "Chapter 2 Bar Graph Example.R" which can be found in the MyFSRrFiles directory.

2.3.2   Producing a Connected Plot for Examining Time-Series Variation

A useful way to get a sense of the variation for a time-series variable is to produce a connected plot in which you display the values of that variable *connected* across time. In the example that we display in Figure 2.1 of *FSR*, we have a connected plot of the values for U.S. presidential approval each month from February 1995 to December 2005. Building on what we learned so far, we will now show you how to produce a figure like this in R. As with the previous example, the first step to doing this is to run commands to load the required packages and the data:

```
library(tidyverse)

load("C:/MyFSRrFiles/presap9505.RData")
```

The command for producing Figure 2.1 of *FSR* is

```
presap9505 %>%
mutate(date_seq = seq(1:nrow(presap9505))) %>%
ggplot(aes(x=date_seq, y=presap)) +
geom_line() +
geom_point() +
theme_bw() +
scale_x_continuous(breaks = seq(6,119, by=6),
labels = presap9505$year_month[seq(6,119, by=6)]) +
ylab("Presidential Approval") +
xlab("Year/Month")
```

This is a fairly complex command which involves first taking the data set that we have loaded, mutating it, and then producing a plot of the resulting data. The "%>%" at the end of the first line of this command tells R that the data object to use is named "presap9505." On the second line of code, it is mutated such that a new variable date_seq is created which is a numeric sequence counting from the top of the first row of data to the bottom. The "`%>%`" at the end of the second line of this command tells R that the resulting data object is now going to be put through another process. In this case, that process is a plot created by `ggplot`. We see an `aes` statement, which is again short for "aesthetic mappings," which tells R that the horizontal axis will be the newly created `date_seq` variable and the vertical axis will be `presap`, which is the Presidential approval variable. The next two lines tell R to create two different graphs, `geom_line()` which is a line graph and `geom_point()` which is a dot plot. The combination of these two graph types shows the exact points of data connected by a line, which is a good way to depict both the individual values of the variable and their progression over time, two essential elements for observing variation across time. The next two lines tell R how to label the horizontal axis, with labels every six months using the original date variable "`year_month`" as the horizontal axis labels. And the last two lines tell R how to label the y and x axes.

All of the commands for this example are contained in a script file called "Chapter 2 Connected Graph Example.R" which can be found in the MyFSRrFiles directory.

2.4 USING GOOGLE SCHOLAR TO SEARCH THE LITERATURE EFFECTIVELY

We assume that you're skilled at web searches, likely using Google's search engine. In addition to the myriad other things that Google allows us to search for on the Internet, it has a dedicated search engine for scholarly publications like books and journal articles. The aspects of Google you're likely most familiar with come from Google's home page, www.google .com. The searches that they enable through scholarly work, however, using what they call "Google Scholar," is at a different site, https:// scholar.google.com. That site looks a good bit like Google's home page, but when you're at Google Scholar, it's searching a different corner of the Internet entirely – the part where academic journals and books are uploaded.

Figure 2.4 shows the Google Scholar home page. If you have a Google account (like a gmail address), you can save items in "My Library" – we'll show you how to do that shortly – that you can access any time. The articles are normally saved as an Adobe .PDF file. You'll notice the familiar search box that looks like Google's normal home page. You can tell from the figure, though, that, despite the similarities in appearances, this website is https://scholar.google.com.

So let's see how Google Scholar works. In the first chapter of *FSR*, we introduced you to what we called the theory of economic threat and attitudes toward immigrants. Let's see what happens when we type "economic threat and attitudes toward immigrants" in the Google Scholar search bar.

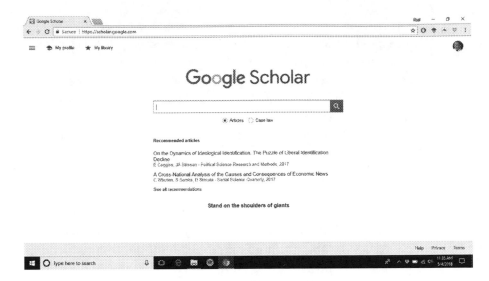

Figure 2.4 The Google Scholar home page

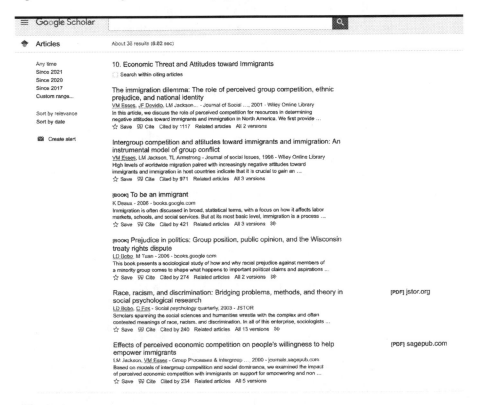

Figure 2.5 Google Scholar results for "economic threat and attitudes toward immigrants" search

Figure 2.5 shows the results of that Google Scholar search. Let's examine that result. If you look to the far right of the fifth selection (the article by Bobo and Fox), you see the text "[PDF] jstor.org," which shows you what format the file is available in – in this case, an Adobe. PDF – and where – in this case, at the archive www.jstor.org. Your college or university's library almost surely has a subscription to JStor that your student fees pay for, and so, if you're on a campus Internet connection (as opposed to a WiFi network at your home, or on a cellular network), clicking on "[PDF] jstor.org" will take you to the article. (If you're on your home WiFi network, then JStor doesn't know that you're a university student, and the publisher might ask you to pay a rather steep fee for access to the article. So beware about where you can do these searches for free.)

There's a lot of other information that the Google Scholar search reveals, though. First, if you want to save an entry to your "My Library," then click on the ☆ at the lower left of the item, and you'll be able to access that .PDF anywhere.

Importantly, you can also see how influential every article has been to date. In Figure 2.5, you can see text near the bottom of the first citation (the article by Esses et al.) that says "Cited by 1117" – which means that the article has been cited 1117 times to date.[3] That number indicates that the paper has been massively influential.[4]

Of course, that doesn't necessarily mean that the 1117 other articles all cite the Esses et al. (2001) article approvingly. Some might; others might not. But being agreed with, or being "proved right," isn't the highest value in science. It's far better to be an influential part of an ongoing debate while being proved wrong in some respects, than it is to be indisputably correct but ignored by other scholars.

Perhaps you say to yourself, "Sure, Esses and her colleagues wrote an influential article on economic threat and attitudes toward immigrants a good long while ago. What kind of work is being done on the topic *now*?" This is one of the places where Google Scholar is fabulous. That "Cited by 1117" is clickable. You can literally see the list of all 1117 articles that cite the Esses article if you want. (Of course, it would take you a while to sift through them!) If you click on "Cited by 1117" and then choose "Since 2017" on the left side of the screens you will see the number of citations that the Esses article has received since 2017. (You can pick "since" any year you like, obviously.) This is a good way to start the process of exploring a particular topic in academic writing that interests you.

---

[3] If you conduct that same search today, the number would surely be higher. Citations tend to accumulate over time.

[4] Of course, you should be careful to remember the original publication date when interpreting citation counts as a measure of impact. The Esses et al. article was published in 2001, so it's not as if some scholars who work in this area have somehow not yet heard of this article. But for an article published more recently – say in 2016 – its impact cannot yet fully be known. That merely means that we don't yet know if the article is likely to have a large impact. Only time will tell.

Just like with using any Internet search engine, there's something of a skill in figuring out how to efficiently search for the material you want without getting bogged down with lots of results that aren't interesting to you. Should you use quotation marks in your search, or in a portion of your search terms? Sometimes yes, sometimes no. (In the example above, we did not.) As a general rule, it might be best to try it both ways to see if you get different results.

We have not exhausted all there is to know about how to use Google Scholar here, of course. For example, many scholars have created "Google Scholar profiles," which enables you to see the list of scholarly articles and books that they have authored, usually sorted from those with the most citations to the ones with the least. This can help you find similar articles, too, because many scholars work on a topic over the course of many years, and therefore their earlier articles are related to their more recent ones. In Figure 2.5, for example, you can see the scholars whose names are underlined; those are clickable links to those scholars' respective Google Scholar profiles. In addition, the "Help" section of Google Scholar is surprisingly helpful!

2.5   WRAPPING UP

In the main FSR text, we discussed how important it is that our theories be new and original – that is, that we aren't merely repeating the ideas and claims of previous scholars. One of the important preconditions for doing something genuinely new is to be familiar with the works that have already been produced on that same topic. Having the vast archive of journal articles and even many books available online – and freely accessible, thanks to your university's libraries – through storage sites like www.jstor.org has been the first step in making this task a lot easier than it was in decades past. The second step has been the invention of very sophisticated search engines like Google Scholar to help us find the previous studies that we otherwise might have missed.

2.6   EXERCISES

1. Conduct a search for the following terms using both Google's home page (www.google.com) and Google Scholar (https://scholar.google.com). Only include the quotation marks in your search if we include them. Report the similarities and differences you observe in the first page of the search results:

(a) "economic threat and attitudes toward immigrants"

(b) economic threat and attitudes toward immigrants

(c) economic threat and prejudice

2. Open the script file named "Chapter 2 Bar Graph Example.R" in RStudio. Make sure that you have the correct directory path for loading the data. In other words, if "C:\MyFSRrFiles" is not where you have your data, change this part of the script file so that the data load into RStudio.

   (a) Once you have done this, follow the steps above to reproduce – as nearly as possible – the graph presented in Figure 2.2 from *FSR*. Open a word processing document and then copy the figure from RStudio and paste it into your word processing document.

   (b) Write a short summary of what you see in this figure.

3. Open the script file named "Chapter 2 Connected Graph Example.R" in RStudio. Make sure that you have the correct directory path for loading the data. In other words, if "C:\MyFSRrFiles" is not where you have your data, change this part of the script so that the data load into RStudio.

   (a) Once you have done this, follow the steps above to reproduce – as nearly as possible – the graph presented in Figure 2.1 from *FSR*. Open a word processing document and then copy the figure from R and paste it into your word processing document.

   (b) Write a short summary of what you see in this figure.

3 Evaluating Causal Relationships

3.1 OVERVIEW

Unlike the previous two chapters, in Chapters 3 through 6, there will not be any computer-based lessons in R. Not to worry, though. There will be more than enough time for intensive computer work later in the book. We promise!

In this abbreviated chapter, then, we offer some expanded exercises that will apply the lessons learned in the main text, and build on the skills from the first two chapters.

3.2 EXERCISES

1. Causal claims are common in media stories about news and politics. Sometimes they are explicitly stated, but often they are implicit. For each of the following news stories, identify the key causal claim in the story, and whether, based on the information given, you are convinced that all four causal hurdles have been crossed. (But remember that most media stories aren't the original generators of causal claims; they merely report on the news as they see fit to do so.)

   (a) www.cnn.com/2018/01/16/politics/freedom-house-democracy-trump-report/index.html

   (b) https://thehill.com/opinion/energy-environment/368355-wheres-the-proof-climate-change-causes-the-polar-vortex

   (c) www.foxnews.com/us/2018/01/16/california-mudslides-where-and-why-happen.html

   (d) www.aljazeera.com/news/2018/01/trump-muslim-ban-shifted-public-opinion-study-finds-180113092728118.html

   (e) www.npr.org/player/embed/575959966/576606076 (Podcast)

2. Candidates for public office make causal claims all the time. For each of the following snippets from a key speech made by a candidate, identify the key causal claim made in the speech, and whether, based on the information given, you are convinced that all four causal hurdles have been crossed. (But remember that candidates for office are not scientists responsible for testing causal claims; they are trying to persuade voters to support them over their opponent.)

(a) "America is one of the highest-taxed nations in the world. Reducing taxes will cause new companies and new jobs to come roaring back into our country. Then we are going to deal with the issue of regulation, one of the greatest job-killers of them all. Excessive regulation is costing our country as much as $2 trillion a year, and we will end it. We are going to lift the restrictions on the production of American energy. This will produce more than $20 trillion in job creating economic activity over the next four decades." (Excerpt from Donald Trump's speech accepting the Republican nomination for President, July 21, 2016.)

(b) "Now, I don't think President Obama and Vice President Biden get the credit they deserve for saving us from the worst economic crisis of our lifetimes. Our economy is so much stronger than when they took office. Nearly 15 million new private-sector jobs. Twenty million more Americans with health insurance. And an auto industry that just had its best year ever. That's real progress." (Excerpt from Hillary Clinton's speech accepting the Democratic nomination for President, July 28, 2016.)

(c) "The truth is, on issue after issue that would make a difference in your lives – on health care and education and the economy – Sen. McCain has been anything but independent. He said that our economy has made 'great progress' under this president. He said that the fundamentals of the economy are strong. And when one of his chief advisers – the man who wrote his economic plan – was talking about the anxiety Americans are feeling, he said that we were just suffering from a 'mental recession,' and that we've become, and I quote, 'a nation of whiners.'" (Excerpt from Barack Obama's speech accepting the Democratic nomination for President, August 28, 2008.)

(d) "His [Barack Obama's] policies have not helped create jobs, they have depressed them. And this I can tell you about where President Obama would take America: His plan to raise taxes on small business won't add jobs, it will eliminate them; ... And his trillion-dollar deficits will slow our economy, restrain employment, and cause wages to stall." (Excerpt from Mitt Romney's speech accepting the Republican nomination for President, August 30, 2012.)

3. Social science, as we have argued, revolves around the making and evaluation of causal claims. Find each of the following research articles – Google Scholar

makes it easy to do so – and then identify the key causal claim made in the article. Then produce a causal hurdles scorecard, and decide to what degree you are convinced that all four causal hurdles have been crossed. Some of the statistical material presented in the articles will, this early in the semester, be beyond your comprehension. That will change as the semester rolls along! (And remember that social scientists are trained to be experts in testing causal claims. So set the bar high.)

(a) Scarborough, W.J., Pepin, J.R., Lambouths III, D.L., Kwon, R., and Monasterio, R. 2021. "The intersection of racial and gender attitudes, 1977 through 2018." *American Sociological Review* 86(5):823–855.

(b) Perry, S.L., Cobb, R.J., Whitehead, A.L., and Grubbs, J.B. 2021. "Divided by faith (in Christian America): Christian nationalism, race, and divergent perceptions of racial injustice." *Social Forces*, soab134, https://doi.org/10.1093/sf/soab134

(c) McLaren, L.M. 2003. "Anti-immigrant prejudice in Europe: Contact, threat perception, and preferences for the exclusion of migrants." *Social Forces* 81(3):909–936.

4 Research Design

OVERVIEW

As was the case in Chapter 3, there will not be any computer-based lessons in R. Again, we offer some expanded exercises that will apply the lessons learned in the main text.

4.2 **EXERCISES**

1. There are a lot of substantive problems in social science that we might *wish* to study experimentally, but which might seem to be impossible to study with experimental methods. (Recall from the main text (Section 4.2.3) that one of the drawbacks to conducting experiments is that not all X variables are subject to experimental control and random assignment.) Imagine the following causal questions, and write a paragraph about what would be required to conduct an experiment in that particular research situation, being careful to refer to both halves of the two-part definition of an experiment in your answer. (Warning: Some of them will seem impossible, or nearly impossible, or might require time travel.)

   (a) Does an individual's religiosity cause a person's level of opposition to same-sex marriage?

   (b) Does a country's openness to trade cause blue-collar workers' wages to fall?

   (c) Does having a more racially diverse set of school administrators and teachers cause a reduction in student suspensions and expulsions?

   (d) Does race cause differences between African American and white girls' experiences in the science classroom?

2. For each of the above research situations, if you were *unable* to perform an experiment, name at least one Z variable that could potentially confound the

$X - Y$ relationship, and would need to be controlled for in some other manner, in an observational study.

3. Assuming that you were unable to conduct an experiment for the aforementioned research situations, describe an observational study that you might conduct instead. In each case, is the study you envision a cross-sectional or time-series observational study? Why?

4. Consider the following research question: Does exposure to stories in the news media shape an individual's opinions on race- and/or gender-related policy issues (e.g., national policies on college admissions, hiring and promoting policies, etc.)?

   (a) Write a short paragraph trying to explain the causal mechanism that might be at work here.

   (b) If we wanted to study this relationship using an experiment, what would the barriers to conducting the experiment be?

   (c) What, if any, are the ethical considerations involved in studying that relationship experimentally?

   (d) What are the benefits of exploring that relationship experimentally? In other words, what specific Z variables would be controlled for in an experiment that could potentially be confounding in an observational study?

   (e) Read the following article and write a one-paragraph summary of it:

   King, G., Schneer, B. and White, A. 2017. "How the news media activate public expression and influence national agendas." *Science* 358:776–780.

5. Consider the relationship between the level of democracy in a country and the country's respect for human rights.

   (a) Describe both a cross-sectional and a time-series observational design that would help test the theory that increases in the level of democracy cause a country to increase its respect for human rights.

   (b) What concerns would you have about crossing the four causal hurdles in each case?

6. Write a one-paragraph summary of the following research articles:

   (a) Branton, R.P., and Jones, B.S. 2005. "Reexamining racial attitudes: The conditional relationship between diversity and socioeconomic environment." *American Journal of Political Science* 49(2):359–372.

   (b) Sullivan, J.M., and Ghara, A. 2015. "Racial identity and intergroup attitudes: A multiracial youth analysis." *Social Science Quarterly* 96(1):261–272.

(c) Bansak, K., Hainmueller, J., and Hangartner, D. 2016. "How economic, humanitarian, and religious concerns shape European attitudes toward asylum seekers." *Science* 354(6309):217–222.

In writing your summaries, address the following questions:

   i. What was the research question/puzzle examined by the author(s)?

  ii. What was their theory?

 iii. What was their research design?

  iv. How did they do with the four hurdles?

   v. What did they conclude?

5 Survey Research

5.1 OVERVIEW

As was the case in Chapters 3 and 4, there will not be any computer-based lessons in R. Again, we offer some expanded exercises that will apply the lessons learned in the main text.

5.2 EXERCISES

1. Select two articles from a social science journal that examine similar topics in an area of research interest to you, one that employs an experimental design and another that uses an observational design.

   (a) Provide a summary of each article, including a description of the dependent variable, the independent variable(s), and any Z variables. What is the primary causal mechanism, according to the authors, that links the independent and dependent variables? Which study do you think provides a more compelling answer to the research question?

   (b) Would it be feasible to combine the experimental and observational designs of the two studies that you selected in an effort to improve upon each?

2. In Exercise 5 in Chapter 1 of *FSR*, we asked you to describe a research question that you might be interested in examining using either the GSS or ANES data sets. We then asked you to describe how that research question might be expanded by using either the ISSP or WVS data sets. In this exercise, visit the website of either the GSS or ANES and the website of either the ISSP or WVS, depending on your selections in Chapter 1. Download to your computer the codebooks for the two data sets that you chose, and identify the variables that you would use to measure your key concepts.

6 Measuring Concepts of Interest

6.1 OVERVIEW

As was the case in Chapters 3, 4, and 5, there will not be any computer-based lessons in R or elsewhere. Again, we offer some expanded exercises that will apply the lessons learned in the main text.

6.2 EXERCISES

1. Consider, for a moment, the concept of "customer satisfaction." For now, let's define it as "the degree to which a product or service meets or exceeds a customer's expectations." So, like other concepts, it is a variable: Some customers are very satisfied, some have mixed experiences, and some are very unhappy. Companies – and even some government agencies – are interested for obvious reasons in understanding that variation. Now answer the following questions:

   (a) How well do you think Yelp reviews serve as a measure of customer satisfaction? Explain your answer.

   (b) Read "The Happiness Button" in the February 5, 2018 issue of *The New Yorker*: www.newyorker.com/magazine/2018/02/05/customer-satisfaction-at-the-push-of-a-button. What are the strengths and weaknesses of the strategy pursued by HappyOrNot in terms of measuring the concept of customer satisfaction?

   (c) The article describes the push-button measures of satisfaction at security checkpoints in London's Heathrow Airport. What are the strengths and weaknesses of such an approach? If, on a particular day, there was a higher share of "frown" responses, what would that tell (and what wouldn't that tell) to the officials at Heathrow?

2. The concept of "religiosity" is a very important one in sociology, as it lies at the heart of many influential theories of why citizens hold the opinions that

they do, including views of racial/ethnic minorities and homosexuality, and why they vote the way that they do. Answer the following questions:

(a) Conceptually, how would you define religiosity? Try to be as specific as possible.

(b) Measuring religiosity, as you might imagine, can be a bit tricky. The flagship specialty journal in the area of the sociology of religion is the *Journal for the Scientific Study of Religion* (hereafter *JSSR*). Go to the website for *JSSR* and search for articles that include "religiosity" in their titles. Read several of them, beginning with the most recent ones and working your way back to earlier issues of the journal. Make a list of the various questions that the authors use in their operational definitions of religiosity and the rationales that they use for doing so. Can you think of an alternative measurement strategy for this concept?

3. The concept of "consumer confidence" is important in the study of economics and political science, among other disciplines.

(a) Go to https://news.google.com and search for "consumer confidence" (and be sure to use the quotation marks). From the search results, pick a recent news article that discusses consumer confidence. (Print out the article and include it with your homework.) How well, if at all, does the article define consumer confidence, or how it is measured?

(b) From what you know, offer a conceptual definition of consumer confidence.

(c) There are two major surveys in the U.S. that measure consumer confidence on monthly intervals. One of them is the Survey of Consumers at the University of Michigan. They produce what they call an Index of Consumer Sentiment, which is composed of responses to five survey items. One of the five is as follows:

> Looking ahead, which would you say is more likely – that in the country as a whole we'll have continuous good times during the next five years or so, or that we will have periods of widespread unemployment or depression, or what?

What are the potential strengths and weaknesses of this survey question as one component of consumer confidence?

(d) All five of the items in the Michigan Index of Consumer Sentiment can be found here: https://data.sca.isr.umich.edu/fetchdoc.php?docid=24770. How are the five items similar to one another, and how are they different from one another?

(e) The complete monthly survey can be found here: https://data.sca .isr.umich.edu/fetchdoc.php?docid=24776. You will note that the survey does not contain *any* questions to measure a survey respondent's political beliefs or affiliations. Why do you think that is the case?

(f) Can you think of any additional survey questions that might complement or replace the ones in the Michigan Index?

7 Getting to Know Your Data

7.1 OVERVIEW

In this chapter we introduce you to the commands needed to produce descriptive statistics and graphs using R in RStudio. If you're feeling a little rusty on the basics of R and RStudio that we covered in Chapters 1 and 2, it would be good to review them before diving into this chapter.

In Chapter 7 of *FSR* we discussed a variety of tools that can be used to get to know your data one variable at a time. In this chapter, we discuss how to produce output in R to allow you to get to know your variables. An important first step to getting to know your data is to figure out what is the measurement metric for each variable. For categorical and ordinal variables, we suggest producing frequency tables. For continuous variables, there are a wide range of descriptive statistics and graphs.

7.2 DESCRIBING CATEGORICAL AND ORDINAL VARIABLES

As we discussed in Chapter 7 of *FSR*, a frequency table is often the best way to numerically examine and present the distribution of values for a categorical or ordinal variable. In R, the "CrossTable" command is used to produce frequency tables. In a script file or from the console command line, the syntax for this command is

```
CrossTable(datasetname$variablename)
```

where *datasetname* is the name of the data set and *variablename* is the name of the variable for which you want the frequencies. When issued like this, this command produces a table with two rows and one column for each unique value for the variable. In the first row, the variable values are displayed and, in the second row, we see the number and the proportion of cases that take on that value in the chosen data set.

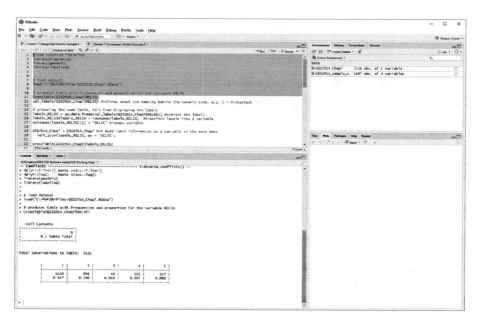

Figure 7.1 Raw output from CrossTable command

The data presented in Table 7.1 of *FSR* are an example of the output obtained from using the "CrossTable" command. These results were generated using the data set GSS2014_sample_chap7.Rdata, which can be found in the R directory at www.cambridge.org/fsr. The output from this use of the CrossTable command is displayed in Figure 7.1. Take a moment to compare the table in Figure 7.1 with Table 7.1 in *FSR*. Although both tables convey the same information, Table 7.1 of *FSR* does so in a more polished fashion. This is an example of why we don't want to copy from the RStudio output and paste that into our papers or presentations. Instead, it is important to craft tables so that they convey what is most necessary and don't include a lot of extra information. We'll have more to say about making tables in Chapter 9 (and forward) in this workbook.

Pie graphs, such as Figure 7.1 in *FSR*, are a graphical way to get to know categorical and ordinal variables. The command to produce a pie graph in a script file or from the console command line using the same data as Figure 7.1 is

```
ggplot(subset(GSS2014_Chap7, !is.na(GSS2014_Chap7$labels_
RELIG)), aes(x="", y=RELIG,
fill=gsub(".*\\.","",labels_RELIG))) +
geom_bar(stat="identity", width=1) +
coord_polar("y", start=0) +
theme_void() +
scale_fill_grey() +
theme(legend.title = element_blank())
```

Figure 7.2 R pie graph

where the first line of code tells R to use only those cases for which the religious self-identification variable (RELIG) is not missing, the second line tells R how to adjust the value labels for this variable,[1] the third line tells R that we are going to produce a type of bar graph, the fourth line tells R that the specific form of bar graph will be displayed on a polar coordinate system (thus a pie graph), the fifth and sixth lines tell R about the theme and colors, and the seventh line tells R how to create the legend. The output in RStudio from this command is displayed in Figure 7.2. It is nearly identical to Figure 7.1 in *FSR*, which was produced in SPSS.

As we discuss is Chapter 7 of *FSR*, statisticians strongly prefer bar graphs to pie charts because bar graphs, especially when they have been sorted by the frequency with which the value occurs, make it easier for one to make assessments about the relative frequency of different values. As an example of how to obtain a figure like this in R, we can run the following code:

```
GSS2014_Chap7 %>% group_by(RELIG) %>%
mutate(count_religion = n()) %>%
dplyr::select(RELIG, count_religion) %>%
```

---

[1] The labels in the data were "1.CATHOLIC," "2.JEWISH," etc. The "gsub" function is for replacing text characters in a data set. So, "gsub" combined with ".*\\." tells R to delete everything before "." and the period. That way, we end up with "CATHOLIC," instead of "1.CATHOLIC."

Figure 7.3 R bar chart

```
distinct() %>%
drop_na() %>%
ggplot(aes(x=reorder(RELIG, -count_religion),
y = count_religion)) +
geom_bar(stat="identity") +
theme_bw()
```

where the first six lines of code rearrange the data objects and the last three produce the bar chart displayed in Figure 7.3. Note, though, that Figure 7.3 is not exactly like Figure 7.2 of *FSR*. To produce this figure, we need the following command:

```
GSS2014_Chap7 %>%
group_by(RELIG) %>%
mutate(count_religion = n()) %>%
dplyr::select(RELIG, count_religion, labels_RELIG) %>%
distinct() %>%
drop_na() %>%
ggplot(aes(x=reorder(gsub(".*\\.","",labels_RELIG),
-count_religion), y
= count_religion)) +
geom_bar(stat="identity") +
theme_bw() +
xlab("") +
ylab("Number of Cases")
```

which adds value labels and a vertical axis label.

7.3   DESCRIBING CONTINUOUS VARIABLES

While the values for categorical variables in a sample of data can easily be presented in a frequency table, this is usually not the case for continuous variables. Consider Table 7.2 in *FSR*. Even for a relatively small data set, such as that presented in Table 7.2 in *FSR*, this output provides a lot of information and it is difficult to see any patterns. For this reason, we turn to summary statistics when we want to describe continuous variables. To use a metaphor, with summary statistics, we are looking at the broad contours of the forest rather than examining each individual tree.

Figure 7.3 in *FSR* displays the output from Stata's "summarize" command with the "detail" option. As we discuss in FSR, this command produces a full battery of descriptive statistics for a continuous variable. To produce similar output in R, we can use the following command:

```
dataset %>%
select(Pct_Own_Home) %>%
drop_na() %>%
summarise(Mean = mean(Pct_Own_Home), SD = sd(Pct_Own_Home),
N = n(),
Min = min(Pct_Own_Home), Max = max(Pct_Own_Home),
Quantiles = quantile(Pct_Own_Home,
c(0, 0.25, 0.5, 0.75, 1)))
```

where the first three lines of code tell R to remove all cases with missing values while making the calculations in the next two lines of code. The results from this code are displayed in Figure 7.4. Note that the mean, standard deviation (SD), minimum (min), and maximum (max) are all repeated in each row and the rank values are displayed in the final column.

While statistical summaries of variables are helpful, it is also quite helpful to also look at visual summaries of the values for a continuous variable. To get a visual depiction of rank statistics, we recommend producing a box–whisker plot like that displayed in Figure 7.4 in *FSR*. The syntax for a box–whisker plot of the values for a single continuous variable (in this case Pct_Own_Home) is

```
ggplot(dataset, aes(y=Pct_Own_Home)) +
geom_boxplot(fill="gray", color="black")
+ theme_bw() + theme(axis.title.x=element_blank(),
axis.text.x=element_blank(), axis.ticks.x=element_blank())
+ ylab("Percentage of African American Homeownership,
1985-2014")
```

To get a visual depiction of moment statistics, we recommend producing either a histogram, such as in Figures 7.5 and 7.6 of *FSR*, or a kernel density plot, such as in Figure 7.7 of *FSR*. The syntax in R for producing a histogram like Figure 7.5 from *FSR* is

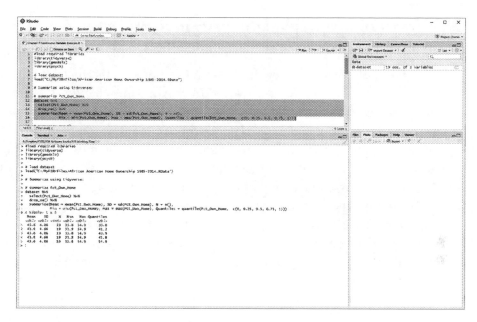

Figure 7.4 R summary statistics

```
ggplot(dataset, aes(x=Pct_Own_Home)) +
geom_histogram(breaks=c(35,40,45,50,55),
aes(y=..density..), colour="black",
fill="gray") +
scale_x_continuous(breaks=c(35,40,45,50,55)) +
theme_bw() +
xlab("Percentage of African American Homeownership,
1985-2014") +
ylab("Density")
```

The syntax in R for producing a density plot like Figure 7.7 from *FSR* is

```
ggplot(dataset, aes(x=Pct_Own_Home)) +
geom_density() +
theme_bw() +
xlab("Percentage of African American Homeownership,
1985-2014") +
ylab("Density")
```

The in syntax R to produce a histogram and density combined in one figure, like in Figure 7.8 from *FSR*, is

```
ggplot(dataset, aes(x=Pct_Own_Home)) +
geom_histogram(breaks=c(35,40,45,50,55),
aes(y=..density..), colour="black", fill="gray") +
scale_x_continuous(breaks=c(35,40,45,50,55))
+ theme_bw() + xlab("Percentage of African American
Homeownership, 1985-2014")
+ ylab("Density") + geom_density()
```

7.4 PUTTING STATISTICAL OUTPUT INTO TABLES, DOCUMENTS, AND PRESENTATIONS

So you've generated some statistical output for the first time. Congratulations! But now what do you do? As you can tell from the descriptions above, we think it's important to be thoughtful about how to present your results to your audience. That's why we went to great lengths to show you commands to make the graphics appear in the most interpretable way possible. The same is true with data that you wish to include in a tabular format. We emphasize that just copying and pasting output from RStudio (or any other program) is unlikely to impress your audience – even if your audience is "just" your professor or teaching assistant.

For example, when we produce descriptive statistics in R, we get a *lot* of output. Usually this output is much more than what we need to present in a paper that describes our variables one at a time. We therefore suggest making your own tables in whatever word processing program you are working with.

Graphs are a bit simpler, though. Once you have a graph that meets the standards we've outlined above, and you want to include in a document, one of the easiest ways to do this is to select the "plot" tab in the lower-left window of RStudio and then click on the button labeled "Export." At this point, you can save your graph as a separate file or choose "copy to clipboard" and then right-click on the location where you want to place the graph in your word processing program and select "paste." Depending on the word processor, you might want to resize the graphic image by clicking on the corner of the image and dragging the image to be bigger or smaller, depending on what would look best in your paper or presentation.

We'll have more to say about this topic in Chapter 9, and forward, as we introduce new statistical techniques to you. The upshot, though, is always the same: put some care into what you present to your audience. The amount of attention you devote to the details – low or high – will be obvious to them.

7.5 EXERCISES

1. Open the script file named "Chapter 7 Categorical Variable Example.R" in RStudio. Make sure that you have the correct directory path for loading the data. In other words, if "C:\MyFSRrFiles" is not where you have your data, change this part of the script file so that the data load into Rstudio.

   Once you have done this, run the code to produce the graphs presented in Figures 7.1 and 7.2 from *FSR*. Open a word processing document and then copy these figures from RStudio and paste them into your word processing document.

2. Run a CrossTable command for variable DEGREE. In your word processing document, create a frequency table like Table 7.1 from *FSR* for variable DEGREE.

3. Create a pie chart and a bar graph like Figures 7.1 and 7.2 from *FSR* for variable DEGREE. Copy these figures from RStudio and paste them into your word processing document.

4. Write a short summary of what you see in the table and figures that you created using variable DEGREE.

5. Open the script file named "Chapter 7 Continuous Variable Example.R" in RStudio. Make sure that you have the correct directory path for loading the data. In other words, if "C:\MyFSRrFiles" is not where you have your data, change this part of the script file so that the data load into RStudio.

   Once you have done this, run the code to create a box–whisker plot, a histogram, a density plot, and a combined histogram and density plot. Copy and paste each of these figures into your word processing document.

8 Probability and Statistical Inference

OVERVIEW

The goal of this chapter is to familiarize you with some of the basics of how probability works, and especially to see how sample sizes come into play. To do this, we take advantage of R's facilities for random number generation.

DICE ROLLING IN R

To simulate rolling a six-sided die and see the results, we can run the following command:

```
sample(1:6, 1, replace=TRUE)
```

which tells R that we want to make a single random draw from whole numbers from 1 to 6. The "sample" function tells R that we wish to randomly generate data, the "1:6" tells R the values from which we want random draws, and then, after a comma, we tell R that we want to sample one value. The statement "replace=TRUE" tells R that we want to do sampling with replacement. Technically, this doesn't matter in this particular instance because we are asking for only a single draw. But, if we were doing multiple draws, this statement would matter. If instead of "replace=TRUE" we wrote "replace=FALSE," we would be sampling without replacement and each number could only be chosen one time. In Figure 8.1 we can see the result from running this command. The result from the depicted single trial, which is displayed in the console window, was a value of "2." Every time you run this command, R will make a new independent draw from whole numbers from 1 to 6.

To see some of the example ideas about probability in action, we can build more complicated simulations. We will start with a simulation of a single six-sided die being rolled sixty times. What should we expect to see

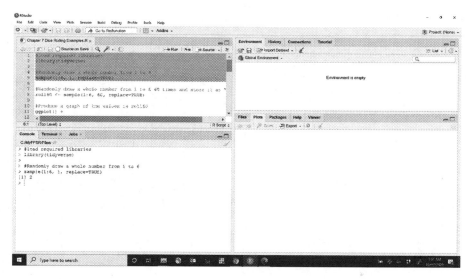

Figure 8.1 Simulating a single roll of a six-sided die

from such a simulation? Because we know that each whole number has an equal probability of being selected on each roll/draw and there are six whole numbers from 1 to 6, we should expect to see each number come up ten times. To run this simulation and look at the results, we issue the following two commands:

```
roll60 <- sample(1:6, 60, replace=TRUE)
```

```
ggplot() +
geom_bar(aes(as.factor(roll60)),
fill = "white", color = "black") +
xlab("roll60")
```

The first command creates a data element, "roll60," which we can see in the "Environment" tab in the upper-right corner of RStudio. That element is generated by the "sample" command after which the only change from our first simulation command is that we change the number of draws from one to sixty.

The results from running these two lines of code are displayed in Figure 8.2. As you can see, we have now changed the number of dice rolls from one to sixty and created a new data element named "roll60" that appears under the "Environment" tab in the upper-right window. As with the previous command, every time we run the first command, the results will change. In this case, the data element roll60 will be replaced, meaning that the distribution of the rolls across the six possible outcomes will vary. The second command, which begins with "ggplot" should be fairly familiar. What it does is create a bar graph of the data element

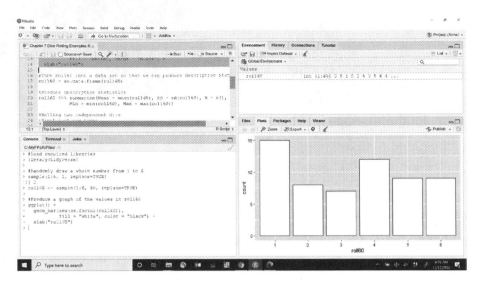

Figure 8.2 Simulating sixty rolls of a six-sided die

roll60 which appears in the lower-right corner of RStudio as depicted in Figure 8.2. The X axis in the figure represents the six sides of the die, and the Y axis represents the number of the rolls that came out with that number. Of course, when you run these commands on your own computer, you will get a different outcome, because the presented results are the result of random forces. In our simulated rolls, however, what you'll notice is that we rolled fewer 3s than we would have expected – seven when we would have expected ten of the rolls to come up 3. Among other things, the figure also reveals that, randomly, we rolled more 1s (fifteen) than would have been predicted by chance. Such is the nature of randomness.

Looking over Figure 8.2, you might have noticed that the entry for the data element roll60 in the "Environment" tab doesn't look like what we saw in that tab for data sets that we loaded into R in earlier chapters. In order to turn it into a data set on which we can calculate descriptive statistics, we need to run the following command:

```
roll60 = as.data.frame(roll60)
```

Now, using what we learned in Chapter 7, we can get R to produce descriptive statistics using the following command:

```
roll60 %>% summarise(Mean = mean(roll60), SD = sd(roll60),
N = n(),
Min = min(roll60), Max = max(roll60))
```

What should we expect for the mean of these sixty rolls?[1] From the lower-right console window in Figure 8.3, we can see that it is 3.32, a little lower

---

[1] The correct answer is 3.5.

Figure 8.3 Descriptive statistics from sixty rolls of a six-sided die

than we expected. The standard deviation – which, as you will recall, measures how tightly clustered or how widely dispersed the scores are – is 1.8.

Using the insights of the central limit theorem from *FSR*, we can use these numbers to create a confidence interval for the likely value of the population mean based on what we have observed in our sample. To do that, we need to calculate the standard error of the mean. You may recall that the formula for the standard error of the mean ($\sigma_{\bar{Y}}$) is

$$\sigma_{\bar{Y}} = \frac{s_Y}{\sqrt{n}},$$

where s_Y is the sample standard deviation and n is the sample size. In our case, that equals

$$\sigma_{\bar{Y}} = \frac{1.8}{\sqrt{60}} = 0.23.$$

To create an approximate 95 percent confidence interval for the likely value of the population mean, you will recall that we can use the rule of thumb that we would go two standard errors in both directions to obtain the interval. In other words:

$$\bar{Y} \pm (2 \times \sigma_{\bar{Y}}) = 3.32 \pm (2 \times 0.23) = 3.32 \pm 0.46.$$

That means, based on what we've observed in our sample, we are 95 percent confident that the population mean for our rolls of the die lies somewhere on the interval between 2.86 and 3.78. And, there is a 2.5 percent chance that the true population mean is below 2.86, and a 2.5 percent chance that the true population mean is above 3.78.

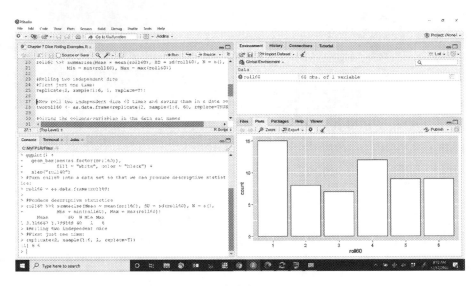

Figure 8.4 Simulating rolling two six-sided dice at once

Of course, you'll be able to tweak this exercise by varying the number of rolls of the die. When you do, it will change that number in the denominator. And, the larger the sample size, the larger the denominator in the formula for the standard error, which means that the resulting quotient will be smaller. That smaller quotient translates to a tighter (smaller) confidence interval. This is how larger sample sizes reduce our uncertainty about the true value of the population characteristics in which we're interested.

Let's do one more example. Say that, instead of rolling one die, we rolled two dice at the same time. What would we expect the sum of the two dice to be?[2] To simulate the rolling of two dice at once, we can use the following command:

```
replicate(2, sample(1:6, 1, replace=T))
```

This tells R that we want to "replicate" the original "sample" command two times. In Figure 8.4, we can see that we rolled two 6s, for a total of 12.

How likely is this outcome?[3] Let's repeat this random draw sixty times to get an approximate answer. We can do this through the following

---

[2] The correct answer is 7.

[3] It's actually highly unlikely and should occur in only one out of thirty-six rolls of two six-sided dice or 2.8 percent of the time.

Figure 8.5 Simulating rolling two six-sided dice at once sixty times

commands (we have left comment notes, preceded by a # symbol, above each command to explain what it does):

```
#Now roll two independent dice 60 times and saving them in
a data set
tworoll60 <- as.data.frame(replicate(2, sample(1:6, 60,
replace=TRUE)))

#Giving the columns/variables in the data set names
colnames(tworoll60) <- c("die 1", "die 2")

#Creating a new variable that is the sum of each pair of
die rolls
tworoll60$sum <- tworoll60$`die 1`+tworoll60$`die 2`

#Plotting the 60 sums
tworoll60 %>% ggplot() +
geom_bar(aes(as.factor(sum)),
fill = "white", color = "black") +
xlab("sum")

#Obtaining descriptive statistics on the sums
tworoll60 %>% summarise(Mean = mean(sum), SD = sd(sum),
N = n(),
Min = min(sum), Max = max(sum))
```

In Figure 8.5, we can see the results from running all of these commands from a script file. In the plot in the lower-right corner, the *x* axis represents the sum of the rolls of the two dice, which has a hypothetical range between 2 and 12. Though, because we did not observe any double 1s, the range in this plot is from 3 to 12. As before, the *y* axis displays the number of rolls in each category. The pattern, we're sure you'll notice, is quite different in Figure 8.5 than it was in Figure 8.2, in which we rolled only one die.

8.3 EXERCISES

1. Open the script file named "Chapter 8 Dice Rollings Examples.R" in RStudio. Write commands to simulate the rolling of a single six-sided die 500 times. Produce a histogram of the output, and calculate the mean and standard deviation of the sample. On the basis of those results, calculate (by hand) the 95 percent confidence interval for the population mean.

2. Make a table with three columns named "die one," "die two," and "sum." In each row, enter one of the possible outcomes of rolling two dice and the sum from that outcome (and note that a 3, 2 is a different outcome than 2, 3). Using this table, do the following:

   (a) Add up all of the entries in the "sum" column and divide by the number of unique outcomes from rolling two dice (the number of rows in your table). Write this number and explain what it is.

   (b) What is the probability of rolling double 6s?

3. Use the commands discussed in this chapter which are located in "Chapter 8 Dice Rollings Examples.R" to show the effects of the sample size on the size of the confidence interval for the population mean by simulating the rolling of two six-sided dice the following number of times:

   (a) nine times

   (b) twenty-five times

   (c) 100 times

   (d) 400 times

   (e) 1600 times

   (f) 2500 times

Describe in some detail the nature of the effects of sample size on the amount of uncertainty we have connecting a sample to the underlying population. *Bonus*: Use RStudio to input data into two variables. Let the first variable be the sample sizes above, and the second variable be the resulting standard error of the mean. Plot the relationship graphically. (*Hint*: You might need to peek ahead to Chapter 9 to see how to do this!)

4. For the above question, how (if at all) does changing the sample size affect the calculated sample means and standard deviations? Can you explain why?

9 Bivariate Hypothesis Testing

9.1 OVERVIEW

We are now ready to start testing hypotheses! As we discuss in Chapter 9 of *FSR*, bivariate hypothesis tests, or hypothesis tests carried out with only two variables, are seldom used as the primary means of hypothesis testing in social science research today. But it is imperative to understand the basic mechanics of bivariate hypothesis tests before moving to more complicated tests. This same logic applies to the use of statistical computing software. In this chapter, we teach you how to conduct hypothesis tests using the four techniques presented in Chapter 9 of *FSR*: tabular analysis, difference of means, the correlation coefficient, and analysis of variance.

9.2 TABULAR ANALYSIS

In tabular analysis, we are testing the null hypothesis that the column variable and row variable are unrelated to each other. We will review the basics of producing a table in which the rows and columns are defined by the values of two different variables, generating hypothesis-testing statistics, and then presenting what you have found.

The R syntax for producing a two-variable table is

```
CrossTable(rowvariable, columnvariable)
```

where "*rowvariable*" is usually the dependent variable (with its values displayed across rows in the table) and "*columnvariable*" is usually the independent variable (with its values displayed down the columns in the table). The values displayed from top to bottom in each cell are as follows: the number of cases, the chi-squared contribution of that cell, the row percentage, the column percentage, and the percentage of total cases. As detailed in Chapter 9 of *FSR*, the column percentages allow

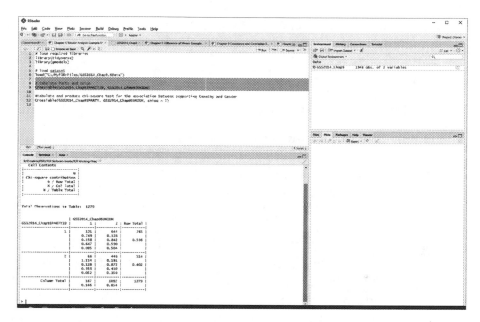

Figure 9.1 Raw output from CrossTable command

for the comparison of interest – they tell us how the dependent variable values differ in terms of their distribution across values of the independent variable.

It is crucial, when working with tables of this nature, to put the appropriate variables across the rows and columns of the table and then to present the column frequencies. For example, to recreate Table 9.2 in *FSR* we first run the command

```
CrossTable(GSS2014_Chap9$PARTYID, GSS2014_Chap9$UNION)
```

where "GSS2014_Chap9" is the data set, "PARTYID" is a categorical variable that takes on a value of "1" if the respondent reported being a Democrat and "2" if the respondent reported being a Republican, and "UNION" is a variable that takes on a value of "1" if the respondent reported that they or their spouse belonged to a union and "2" otherwise.

The output from this running command is displayed in Figure 9.1. Take a moment to compare this raw output with Table 9.2 in *FSR*. There are three notable differences. First, in order to isolate the numbers needed for the assessment at hand (whether or not respondents from union households were affiliated with political parties differently from respondents from nonunion households), we need only the column percentages. Second, instead of the names of the variables from the output ("PARTYID" and "UNION") and the numbers reflecting their values ("1" and "2"), we have provided more intuitive labels for the variables and their values. And, third, we have added a note making it clear what are the values reported in each cell of the table.

9.2.1 Generating Test Statistics

In Chapter 9 of *FSR* we discuss in detail the logic of Pearson's chi-squared test statistic which we use to test the null hypothesis that the row and column variables are not related. To get this test statistic and the associated *p*-value for a two-variable table in R we can use the following command:

```
CrossTable(rowvariable, columnvariable, chisq = T)
```

where, again, "*rowvariable*" is usually the dependent variable (with its values displayed across rows in the table) and "*columnvariable*" is usually the independent variable (with its values displayed down the columns in the table). The ", chisq = T" (which is shorthand for Chi-squared=True) tells R to report a chi-squared test statistic and the associated *p*-value. Thus to conduct the chi-squared test for our current example, we would issue the command

```
CrossTable(GSS2014_Chap9$PARTYID, GSS2014_Chap9$UNION,
chisq = T)
```

which produces the output displayed in Figure 9.2. The calculated value of the chi-squares statistic is 2.182 – you could do it by hand following

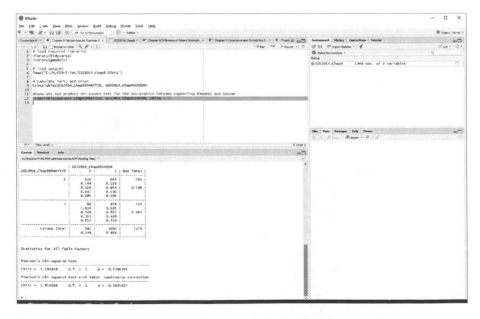

Figure 9.2 Raw output from CrossTable command with a chi-squared test

the formula in Chapter 9 of the main text – and the associated p-value is 0.14. Because that is greater than 0.05, the relationship is not statistically significant, meaning that it very likely does not exist in the underlying population from which the sample was drawn.

9.2.2 Putting Tabular Results into Papers

We recommend that you make your own tables in whatever word processing program you choose to use instead of copying and pasting the tables that you make in RStudio. The first reason for doing so is that you will think about your results more closely when you are producing your own tables. This will help you to catch any mistakes that you might have made and to write more effectively about what you have found. Another reason for doing so is that tables constructed by you will tend to look better. By controlling how the tables are constructed, you will be able to communicate with maximum clarity.

As a part of making your own tables, you should have the goal in mind that your table communicates something on its own. In other words, if someone *only* looked at your table, would they be able to figure out what was going on? If the answer is "yes," then you have constructed an effective table. We offer the following advice ideas for making useful tables:

- Give your tables a title that conveys the essential result in your table.
- Make your column and row headings as clear as possible.
- Put notes at the bottom of your tables to explain the table's contents.

9.3 DIFFERENCE OF MEANS

Difference of means tests are conducted when we have a continuous dependent variable and a limited independent variable.

9.3.1 Examining Differences Graphically

When we use graphs to assess a difference of means, we are graphing the distribution of the continuous dependent variable for two or more values of the limited independent variable. Figure 9.1 of *FSR* shows how this is done with a box–whisker plot. The code for producing a figure like Figure 9.1 of *FSR* is[1]

---

[1] The figure in *FSR* was created using Stata, so there will be some slight differences between that and what you produce using R in RStudio.

```
ggplot(GSS2000_2014r1, aes(x=as.factor(raceeth1) ,y=EDUC)) +
geom_boxplot(fill="gray", color="black") +
scale_x_discrete(labels = c("White", "Black")) +
theme_bw() +
xlab("") +
ylab("Highest year of school completed")
```

where the variable "`raceeth1`" is the respondent's race (divided into non-Hispanic black and non-Hispanic whites only) and "`EDUC`" is the years of education.

9.3.2 Generating Test Statistics

To conduct a difference of means t-test such as the one discussed in Chapter 9 of *FSR*, the syntax is[2]

```
t.test(EDUC ~as.factor(raceeth1), data = GSS2000_2014r1,
var.equal = T)
```

which produces the output displayed in the console window in the bottom-left corner of Figure 9.3. From this output, we can see the calculated $t = 15.946$, which is statistically significant ($p < 0.001$).

Figure 9.3 Raw output from a difference of means test

---

[2] The contents inside the first set of parentheses in this command after "t.test" tells R the name of the dependent variable, and, after the "~", the name of the independent variable. The "as.factor" lets R know that the independent variable is a categorical variable.

9.4 CORRELATION COEFFICIENTS

Correlation coefficients summarize the relationship between two continuous variables. They are also an important building block to understanding the basic mechanics of two-variable regression models.

9.4.1 Producing Scatter Plots

We can examine the relationship between two continuous variables in a scatter plot such as Figure 9.3 in *FSR*. We can reproduce the main features of this figure with the following command:

```
ggplot(GovtAsst, aes(x=Unempl, y=GovtAsst)) +
geom_point() +
theme_bw()
```

where "geom_point()" tells R that we want to produce a scatter plot. The results from this command are displayed in the plot window in the lower-right part of Figure 9.4. The command for producing Figure 9.3 in *FSR* is[3]

```
ggplot(GovtAsst, aes(x=Unempl, y=GovtAsst)) +
geom_point(shape=1) +
theme_bw() +
```

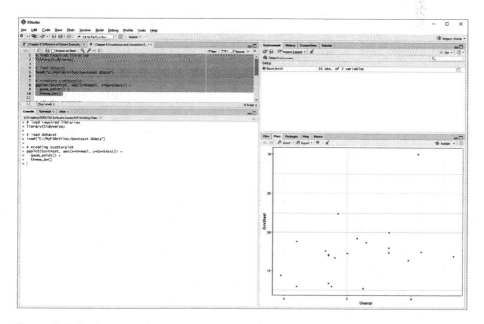

Figure 9.4 Basic output from scatter command

[3] The figure in *FSR* was created using Stata, so there will be some slight differences between that and what you produce using R in RStudio.

```
xlab("Unemployment Rate") +
ylab("Percentage Support for Government Assistance to the
Poor")
```

where "`geom_point(shape=1)`" tells R to make hollow circles instead of the default filled-in circles that we see in Figure 9.4. These open symbols make it a little bit easier to see overlapping data points.

9.4.2   Generating Covariance Tables and Test Statistics

To generate the output for a covariance table like Table 9.11 in *FSR*, the command is

```
cov(GovtAsst[, c("GovtAsst", "Unempl")],
use = "complete.obs")
```

To generate a correlation coefficient using these same variables, the command is

```
cor(GovtAsst[, c("GovtAsst", "Unempl")],
use = "complete.obs")
```

And to calculate the *t*-test presented in *FSR*, the command is

```
cor.test(GovtAsst$GovtAsst, GovtAsst$Unempl,
use = "complete.obs")
```

which generates the output that we see in Figure 9.5.

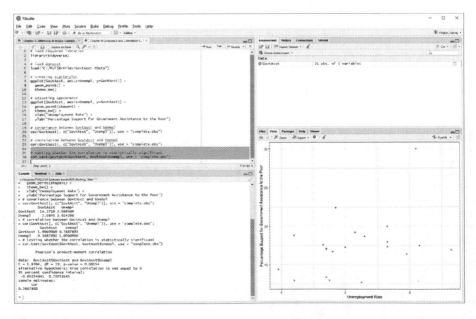

Figure 9.5 Output from cor.test command

9.5 ANALYSIS OF VARIANCE

Our final example of bivariate hypothesis testing is analysis of variance, or ANOVA for short. As Table 9.1 in *FSR* shows, ANOVA models, like difference of means tests, require a continuous dependent variable and a categorical independent variable. However, as we discuss in Section 9.4.4 of *FSR*, ANOVA, unlike difference of means tests, is appropriate when the independent variable has three or more, rather than just two, categories.

9.5.1 Examining Differences Graphically

As we did earlier in this chapter (Section 9.3) for a continuous dependent variable and an independent variable with two categories, in this section we illustrate how to graphically analyze a continuous dependent variable and an independent variable with three categories. The data set we use is "GSS2000_2014r2.RData." As usual, these data are located in the "MyFSRrFiles" folder created for this workbook. The command for creating a box–whisker plot for this analysis is

```
ggplot(GSS2000_2014r2, aes(x=as.factor(raceeth2),
y=EDUC)) +
geom_boxplot(fill='deepskyblue4', color="black") +
scale_x_discrete(labels=c("1" = "Non Hispanic White",
"2" = "Non Hispanic Black", "4" = "Hispanic")) +
labs(title="Simple Boxplot for Highest year of school
completed by
raceeth2", x ="Race/Ethnicity",
y = "Highest year of school completed") +
theme_classic()
```

This command produces the plot displayed in the lower-right corner of Figure 9.6.

9.5.2 Generating ANOVA Test Statistics

To generate the relevant descriptive statistics for the ANOVA test, we can use the following command:

```
GSS2000_2014r2 %>%
group_by(raceeth2) %>%
summarize(N = n(),
Mean = mean(EDUC,na.rm=T),
SD = sd(EDUC,na.rm=T),
Minimum = min(EDUC,na.rm=T),
Maximum = max(EDUC,na.rm=T),
)
```

This command produces the output displayed in the lower-left corner of Figure 9.7.

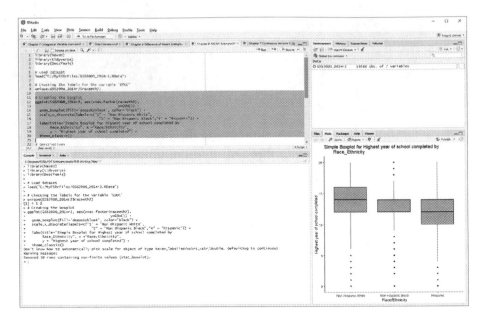

Figure 9.6 Box–whisker plot of racial/ethnic differences in education

Figure 9.7 ANOVA descriptive statistics

From the descriptive statistics displayed in Figure 9.7, we can see the average number of years of education completed for each group. Are these means large enough to warrant rejection of our null hypothesis of no racial/ethnic group differences in educational attainment in the underlying population? To answer this question we must conduct an ANOVA test. To

Figure 9.8 ANOVA output

conduct an analysis of variance test such as the one discussed in Chapter 9 of *FSR* and to produce the output displayed in Table 9.12 of *FSR*, you can use the following two commands:

```
model = lm(EDUC   as.factor(Race_Ethnicity),
data = GSS2014_Sample_Chap9_ANOVA)
summary(model)


anova.test = aov(model)
summary(anova.test)
```

These commands produce the output displayed in the lower-left corner of Figure 9.8. Look at the final lines of output – specifically, to the last column of the first row of output where the *p*-value is reported. Since that value is less than 0.05, we can reject the null hypothesis of equality of population means in favor of the alternative hypothesis that at least one mean (or means) is (are) different from at least one other mean (or means). But which ones are different from which others?

In order to answer this important question, we have to take one additional step. In order to do so we conduct what is referred to as a multiple comparison procedure. The command for this is

```
ScheffeTest(anova.test)
```

which produces the output displayed in the lower left of Figure 9.9. An examination of this output shows that each of the group means is significantly different from each of the other group means. In other words,

Figure 9.9 Output from a Scheffe ANOVA multiple comparison test procedure

non-Hispanic whites have significantly higher educational attainment than both non-Hispanic blacks and Hispanics; non-Hispanic blacks have significantly lower educational attainment than non-Hispanic whites but significantly higher educational attainment than Hispanics; and Hispanics are significantly lower on educational attainment than both whites and blacks.

9.6 EXERCISES

1. Launch RStudio and load the "GSS2014_Sample_Chap9_v5.RData" data set. Once you have done this, conduct a chi-squared test of the null hypothesis that sex and party are statistically independent. Discuss your results.

2. Using the same data set, perform a difference of means test using sex as the independent variable and education as the dependent variable. Discuss your results.

3. Launch RStudio and open the "GovtAsst.RData" data set. Once you have done this, output a correlation matrix showing the relationship between unemployment rate and attitudes toward government assistance toward the poor. Discuss your results.

10 Two-Variable Regression Models

10.1 OVERVIEW

In Chapter 10 of *FSR* we introduce the two-variable regression model. As we discuss, this is another two-variable hypothesis test that amounts to fitting a line through a scatter plot of observations on a dependent variable and an independent variable. In this chapter, we walk you through how to estimate such a two-variable model in R using RStudio.

10.2 ESTIMATING A TWO-VARIABLE REGRESSION

The estimation of a two-variable regression model, as discussed in Chapter 10 of *FSR*, is fairly straightforward. The syntax is

```
ModelName = lm(DependentVariable ~IndependentVariable,
data = DataSet)
```

where "*ModelName*" is the name you give to your model, "*lm*" is the command which tells R to estimate a regression model, "*DependentVariable*" is the name of the dependent variable, "*IndependentVariable*" is the name of the independent variable, and "*DataSet*" is the name of the data set, which must be loaded into RStudio, on which we want to estimate the regression model. Having estimated our model with such a command, there will now be a new data element called whatever you chose for "*ModelName*" which contains all of the results from the model that you estimated. To see the main results from your model, you need to run the following new command:

```
summary(ModelName)
```

So, to estimate the model of opinions on government assistance to the poor as a function of economic conditions (unemployment) that we

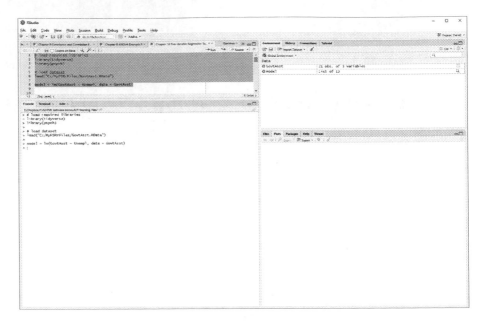

Figure 10.1 RStudio after the estimation of a two-variable regression model

feature so prominently in Chapter 10 of *FSR*, you would run the following command:

```
model = lm(GovtAsst ~Unempl, data = GovtAsst)
```

Figure 10.1 shows what RStudio looks like after this command has been successfully submitted. This is very different from what we would expect to see if we were estimating a regression model in most other statistical software programs. In most programs, we would expect to see a bunch of numerical output like what we see in Figure 10.4 of *FSR*. One thing that you might have noticed is that in Figure 10.1 there is a data element named "model" under the "Environment" tab in the upper-right part of the RStudio window.

In order to produce output such as that pictured in Figure 10.4 of *FSR*, we need to run a summary command, in this case

```
summary(model)
```

which tells R to present output from the model. The output from this model is now displayed in the console window in the lower-left part of Figure 10.2.

10.3   GRAPHING A TWO-VARIABLE REGRESSION

To better understand what is going on in a two-variable regression model, it is often helpful to graph the regression line. An example of this is

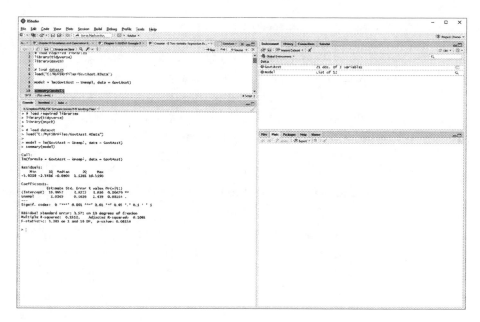

Figure 10.2 Model summary output for a two-variable regression

presented in Figure 10.3 of *FSR*. The code for producing a figure very similar to this in R is

```
GovtAsst %>%
mutate(fitted = as.numeric(fitted(model))) %>%
ggplot(aes(x=Unempl)) +
geom_point(aes(y = GovtAsst) )+
geom_line( aes(y=fitted, group=1,)) +
theme_bw() +
theme(legend.title=element_blank()) +
xlab("Unemployment Rate") +
ylab("Percentage Support for Government Assistance to
the Poor") +
geom_hline(yintercept=mean(GovtAsst$GovtAsst),
linetype="dashed") +
geom_vline(xintercept=mean(GovtAsst$Unempl),
linetype="dashed")
```

10.4 EXERCISES

1. Open the script file named "Chapter 10 Two-Variable Regression Examples.R" in RStudio. Make sure that you have the correct directory path for loading the data. In other words, if "C:\MyFSRrFiles" is not where you have your data, change this part of the script file so that the data load into RStudio. Once you have done this, run the code to produce Figure 10.3 from *FSR*. Copy and paste this figure into your word processing document.

2. If we change the independent variable in our running example from "unemployment" to "year," what would the theory of economic threat lead us to expect in terms of a hypothesis for the slope of a regression line with variable "GovtAsst" as the dependent variable and "year" as the independent variable? Explain your answer.

3. Estimate a regression model with the variable "GovtAsst" as the dependent variable and "year" as the independent variable.

   (a) Copy and paste this output into your word processing document.

   (b) Write about the results from the hypothesis test that you discussed above. What does this tell you about the theory of economic threat?

   (c) Produce a figure like Figure 10.3 from *FSR* but with year as the independent variable (GovtAsst should remain as the dependent variable). Copy and paste this figure into your word processing document.

11 Multiple Regression

11.1 OVERVIEW

In Chapter 11 of *FSR*, we introduce the multiple regression model in which we are able to estimate the effect of X on Y holding Z constant. Here, we show you how to work with such models in R.

11.2 ESTIMATING A MULTIPLE REGRESSION

The estimation of a multiple regression model, as discussed in Chapter 11 of *FSR*, is just an extension of the command used for estimating a two-variable regression. For example, if we have three independent variables, the syntax is

```
ModelName = lm(DependentVariable ~IndependentVariable1 +
IndependentVariable2 + IndependentVariable3, data =
DataSet)
```

where "*DependentVariable*" is the name of the dependent variable, and the terms that begin with "*IndependentVariable*" are the names of the independent variables.[1] For R's multiple regression command, the name of the dependent variable must always come first, followed by the names of the independent variables after the ~. The order in which the independent variables appear does not matter; you will get the same results regardless of their order.

---

[1] In this example of the syntax, we have chosen to show the syntax for having three independent variables. In practice, you may have as many independent variables as you want in a regression model as long as you meet the minimum mathematical requirements that each independent variable varies, $n > k$, and you have no perfect multicollinearity. The first two of these requirements are discussed in Section 10.5.3 and the third is discussed in Section 11.8.1 of *FSR*.

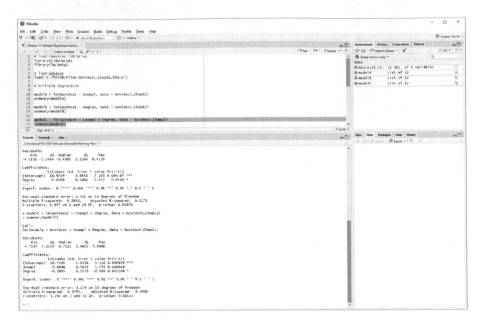

Figure 11.1 Basic output from a multiple regression

The commands to estimate the multiple regression displayed under the column titled "C" in Table 11.3 of *FSR* and to display the results from it are

```
modelC = lm(GovtAsst ~Unempl + Degree, data =
GovtAsst_Chap11)
summary(modelC)
```

Running this command produces the output which is displayed in the bottom left of Figure 11.1.

11.3 FROM REGRESSION OUTPUT TO TABLE – MAKING ONLY ONE TYPE OF COMPARISON

As we discuss in Section 12.4 of *FSR*, when presenting the results from more than two regression models in the same table, it is important that we set up our comparisons appropriately – either as comparisons of different model specifications estimated with the same sample of data, or as the same model specification estimated with different samples of data. This is because if both the sample of data and the model specification change, then we cannot know for sure whether any differences in the estimates that we are observing are due to the different sample or the different specification.

11.3.1 Comparing Models with the Same Sample of Data, but Different Specifications

If your data set doesn't have any missing values for any of the variables that you want to include in a set of models with different specifications, then making a table for such comparisons is pretty straightforward. All that you need to do is to estimate the regressions of interest to you and put them into separate columns of a table. If, as is often the case, you have some missing values for some of the variables that you are including in your different models, then you need to take some extra steps in order to make sure that the regressions that you are comparing are all estimated with the exact same observations.

As an example of this, let's assume that the variable "Degree" is missing for the year 2010. Since regression models are based on only those cases that have no missing data on any of the variables in the model, it would be necessary for us to exclude the year for which the degree variable was missing. Given that we know the year of the observation that we want to exclude, we can simply tell R to select all cases where the value of the variable "year" is not equal to 2010.

One way to do this, given that we know the year of the observation that we want to exclude would be to write the command as

```
modelB1 = lm(GovtAsst ~Unempl,
data = GovtAsst_Chap11, GovtAsst_Chap11$Year!=2010)
```

which tells R to estimate a regression with `GovtAsst` as the dependent variable and `Degree` as the independent variable using *only* that "`subset`" of observations for which the variable year is not equal to 2010 ("`year!=2010`" where "`!=`" means "is not equal to").

But what would we do if we didn't know exactly which observations are missing particular values of particular independent variables?[2] One of the easiest ways is just to estimate the model using all cases that are not missing for any of the independent variables that you plan to include in the models that you want to present. In our running example, we would estimate the following two models:

```
modelA2 = lm(GovtAsst ~Unempl,
data = subset(GovtAsst_Chap11,
!(is.na(GovtAsst_Chap11$Degree))))
```

[2] If an observation is missing for the dependent variable, it will not be included in any of the models that we estimate. Also, in general, we should have gotten to know our data before we estimate a regression model, and part of getting to know one's data is figuring out what are the missing values and why they are missing.

```
modelB2 = lm(GovtAsst ~Degree,
data = subset(GovtAsst_Chap11,
!(is.na(GovtAsst_Chap11$Unempl))))
```

where the "!(is.na" means "is not missing."

11.3.2   Comparing Models with the Same Specification, but Different Samples of Data

As an example of how to compare models with the same specification, but different samples of data, let's imagine that we want to look at the results from our running example of support for government assistance to the poor for observations after the turn of the twenty-first century compared with all observations before then. So, to estimate models on samples of data beginning in 2000 and all other cases, we would estimate the following two models:

```
modelC3a = lm(GovtAsst   Unempl + Degree, data =
subset(GovtAsst_Chap11, Year<2000))
```

```
modelC3b = lm(GovtAsst   Unempl + Degree, data =
subset(GovtAsst_Chap11, Year>1999))
```

where the commands are identical except for the conditions written after the "subset."

11.4   STANDARDIZED COEFFICIENTS

In order to obtain standardized coefficients, as discussed in Section 11.6 of *FSR*, we would first estimate the model normally:

```
modelC = lm(GovtAsst ~Unempl + Degree, data =
GovtAsst_Chap11)
summary(modelC)
```

and then run the command

```
lm.beta(model1)
```

which will produce the output displayed in Figure 11.2.

11.5   DUMMY VARIABLES

As we discuss in Section 11.9 of *FSR*, dummy variables are categorical variables that take on one of two different values. The vast majority of

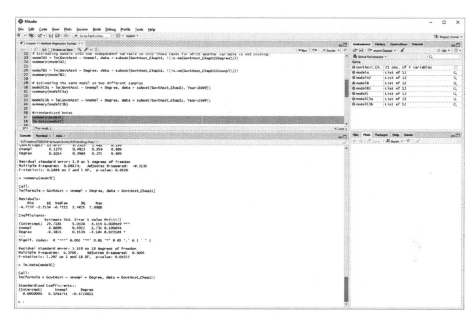

Figure 11.2 Basic output from a multiple regression with the "beta" coefficients

the time in sociology, political science, and other social sciences, these two values are "zero" and "one." Dummy variables are usually created and named so that "one" represents the presence of a condition and "zero" represents the absence of that condition. In order to not confuse the people who will be reading your work or watching your presentations, it is a good idea to follow these conventions. For example, if you have a dummy variable to identify the gender identity of a survey respondent, it might be tempting to call the variable "gender." That, however, would leave unclear the issue of what the zeros and ones represent. If, by contrast, you named your variable "female," then the convention would be that a zero is for male respondents – or the absence of the condition "female" – and one is for the female respondents – the presence of the condition "female."

11.5.1 Creating a Dummy Variable in R

Sometimes data sets that you are working with come with proper dummy variables already created for you. When they do not, you will need to create your own variables. As an example of this, we will work with the data file "GSS2016_Sample_Chap11.RData."

From the codebook for this study, we can tell that coding of values for each respondent's self-identified gender is in the variable named "SEX," and that the values of this variable are equal to 1 for "male" and 2 for "female." Here are the commands in which we create a new dummy variable:

```
GSS2016_Sample_Chap11 = GSS2016_Sample_Chap11 %>%
mutate(female = ifelse(SEX==1, 0, 1))
```

which tells R on the first line to start with the data set "GSS2016_Sample_Chap11," which is a subset of the 2016 GSS. On the second line, we create a new dummy variable using a combination of "mutate" and "ifelse." As we've seen before, "mutate" tells R that we are going to change something. The "ifelse" statement is a function that tells R to test a logical argument and, if it is true, to do 1 thing and, if the logical argument is not true, to do something else. So this line of code tells R to create a new variable named "female" and, if SEX is equal to 1 to make female equal to 0, and otherwise to make it equal to 1.

Whenever you create a new variable, it is critically important to check that you created exactly what you intended to create. One way to check this is with a CrossTable command which we introduced in Chapter 9 of this companion. In this case, we could check our work with the command:

```
CrossTable(GSS2016_Sample_Chap11$SEX,
GSS2016_Sample_Chap11$female)
```

which tells R to create a two-variable table with the values of "SEX" and "female." From the results in the console window of Figure 11.3, we can see that we did create the variable that we wanted.

11.5.2 Estimating a Multiple Regression Model with a Single Dummy Independent Variable

As we discussed in Section 11.2 of this software companion book, the syntax for estimating a multiple regression with three independent variables is:

```
ModelName = lm(DependentVariable ~IndependentVariable1 +
IndependentVariable2 + IndependentVariable3,
data = DataSet)
```

where "DependentVariable" is the name of the dependent variable, and the "IndependentVariable" terms are the names of the three independent variables. When we have only a single dummy independent variable, then we just simply add the name of that variable to the list after the "~".

As an example of this, we can estimate the regression model displayed on the left side of Table 11.4 of *FSR* with the following command:

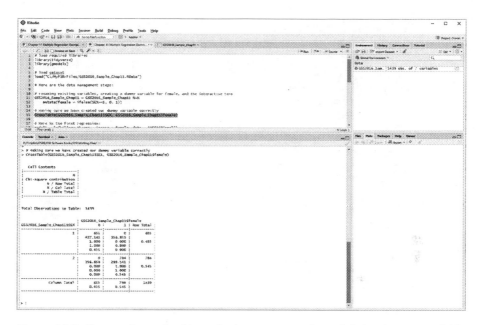

Figure 11.3 Output from checking whether we correctly coded the dummy variable "female"

```
model1 = lm(RINCOM16 ~female + EDUC,
data - GSS2016_Sample_Chap11)
```

where "RINCOM16" is the dependent variable, a respondent's income, "EDUC" is a continuous independent variable, and "female" is the dummy independent variable that we just created. Note that, as was the case with our multiple regression models with multiple continuous independent variables, the order of the independent variables does not matter for this command. The output from this model is displayed in Figure 11.4.

11.5.3 Estimating a Multiple Regression Model with Multiple Dummy Independent Variables

To estimate a multiple regression model with multiple dummy variables, you use the same procedure as in the previous section. The main complication comes when the multiple dummy variables represent values for a categorical variable with more than two values. As we discuss in Section 11.9.1 of *FSR*, in such a case, in order to avoid what is known as the "dummy variable trap," you need to leave one category of such an independent variable out of the regression model, and that left-out category becomes the "reference category."

Figure 11.4 Output from a regression model with a dummy variable

11.6 DUMMY VARIABLES IN INTERACTIONS

In Section 11.10 of *FSR*, we discuss testing interactive hypotheses with dummy variables. There are several different ways to do this in R. We recommend that you use a fairly straightforward approach where you start out by creating a new variable that is the multiplicative interaction between the dummy independent variable and the continuous independent variable. We'll again follow along the example from that section of the main text.

In order to create the interactive model displayed on the right side of Table 11.9 of *FSR*, we first create the interaction between the continuous variable "EDUC" (the respondents' educational levels), and the dummy variable "male" with the following command:

```
GSS2016_Sample_Chap11 = GSS2016_Sample_Chap11 %>%
mutate(male_EDUC=male*EDUC)
```

We can then estimate the model displayed on the right side of Table 11.9 of *FSR* with the following command:

```
model2 = lm(RINCOM16 ~male + EDUC + male_EDUC, data =
GSS2016_Sample_Chap11)
```

11.7 MODELS WITH DUMMY DEPENDENT VARIABLES

As we discuss in Chapter 11 of *FSR*, there are several different models that can be used when we have a dummy dependent variable. In this set

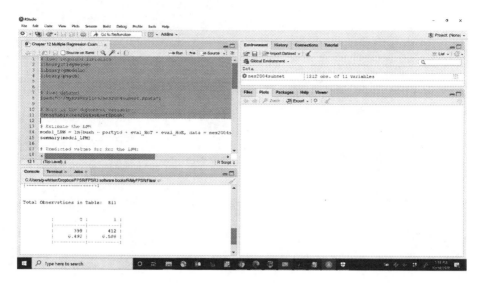

Figure 11.5 Table of values for the variable "Bush"

of examples, we will work with data from the 2004 American National Election Study (ANES) with a dependent variable named "Bush," which equals 1 for respondents who reported that they voted for George W. Bush and equals 0 for those respondents who reported that they voted for John Kerry.[3] To get a look at the values for this variable, we can run a CrossTable command

```
CrossTable(nes2004subset$bush)
```

which produces the output displayed in Figure 11.5. As we discuss in Chapter 11 of *FSR*, one option when we have a limited dependent variable is simply to estimate a regression model using the standard syntax that we discussed in Chapter 10 of this companion. For example, if we have three independent variables, the command is

```
ModelName = lm(DependentVariable ~IndependentVariable1 +
IndependentVariable2 + IndependentVariable3, data = DataSet)
```

and the only difference is that the DependentVariable is a dummy variable. So, if we want to estimate the model displayed in Table 11.10 of *FSR*, we would write the command as

```
model_LPM = lm(bush ~partyid + eval_WoT + eval_HoE,
data = nes2004subset)
```

where "bush" is the dependent variable for which the values are displayed in Figure 11.5, "partyid" is "Party Identification," "eval_WoT" is

---

[3] This is the same example that we use in Chapter 11 of *FSR*. For a more detailed explanation of the variable and how it was created, see footnote 19 at the beginning of Section 11.11.1 of *FSR*.

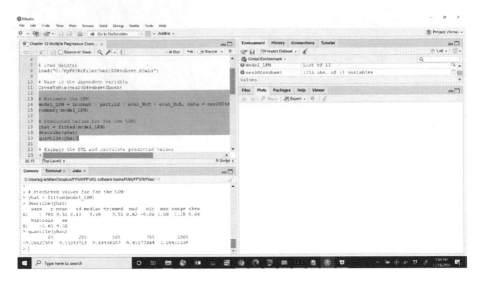

Figure 11.6 Calculating and displaying the predicted values from the linear probability model

"Evaluation: War on Terror," and "`eval_HoE`" is "Evaluation: Health of the Economy." To calculate and summarize the predicted probabilities from this model, we use the following commands with what should now be familiar syntax

```
yhat = fitted(model_LPM)
describe(yhat)
quantile(yhat)
```

which produces the output displayed in Figure 11.6. If we look at the results from these commands, we can see that we get some predicted values (what we refer to as $\hat{P}_i$ values) that are greater than 1 and some that are less than 0. As we discuss in Chapter 11 of *FSR*, one of the problems of the linear probability model is that it can produce predicted probabilities that are greater than 1 or less than 0. This is one of the main reasons why some researchers prefer to use either a binomial logit (BNL) model or a binomial probit (BNP) model when they have a dummy dependent variable.

To estimate a binomial logit model in R, the syntax is

```
ModelName = glm(DependentVariable ~IndependentVariable1 +
IndependentVariable2 + IndependentVariable3, data = DataSet,
family = binomial(link = "logit"))
```

and to estimate a binomial probit model in R, the syntax is

```
ModelName = glm(DependentVariable ~IndependentVariable1 +
IndependentVariable2 + IndependentVariable3, data = DataSet,
family = binomial(link = "probit"))
```

As we discuss in Chapter 11 of *FSR*, with each of these types of models there is an estimated systematic component for each observation, what we call the $X_i\hat{\beta}$ values, that can be put through a link function to produce predicted probabilities, what we refer to as $\hat{P}_i$ values. The command for calculating the $\hat{P}_i$ values after either a binomial logit or binomial probit has been estimated is

```
newvariable=fitted(ModelName)
```

where "*newvariable*" is the name of the new variable that we want to create, and the "fitted" tells R that we want the new variable to be the predicted probabilities for each of our observations that was included in the model estimation.

So, to continue with our running example, we can produce the logit and probit columns of the results displayed in Table 11.11 of *FSR* and predicted probabilities for each observation by running the following lines of code

```
model_BNL = glm(bush ~partyid + eval_WoT + eval_HoE,
data = nes2004subset,
family = binomial(link = "logit"))
summary(model_BNL)
p_BNL = fitted(model_BNL)

model_BNP - glm(bush   partyid + eval_WoT + eval_HoE,
data = nes2004subset,
family = binomial(link = "probit"))
summary(model_BNP)
p_BNP = fitted(model_BNP)
```

We can then display summary statistics for the resulting predicted probabilities by running the following lines of code

```
describe(p_BNL)
quantile(p_BNL)
describe(p_BNP)
quantile(p_BNP)
```

which produces the output presented in Figure 11.7.

In order to produce classification tables like Table 11.12 in *FSR*, we need to first create a new variable, which is the predicted value of the dependent variable, what we have labeled "Model-based expectations" in Table 11.12. For the linear probability model in this example, we would use the following lines of code:

```
nes2004subset_2 = nes2004subset %>%
select(bush, partyid, eval_WoT, eval_HoE) %>%
drop_na() %>%
mutate(p_vote_lpm = ifelse(yhat>0.5, 1, 0),
p_vote_bnl = ifelse(p_BNL>0.5, 1, 0),
p_vote_bnp = ifelse(p_BNP>0.5, 1, 0))
```

where we first create a new variable p_vote_lpm equal to the predicted values from the linear probability model that we estimated. We then recode

Figure 11.7 Summary statistics for predicted values from a binomial logit model and a binomial probit model

Figure 11.8 Raw output used to produce Table 11.12 of *FSR*

the values of `p_vote_lpm` so that predicted probabilities of 0.5 or smaller become predictions that the individual will vote for Kerry (coded as 0) and predicted probabilities greater than 0.5 become predictions that the individual will vote for Bush (coded as 1). We then produce a table of the values of actual vote and our model-based predictions. The output from these commands is presented in Figure 11.8.

11.8 EXERCISES

1. Open the script file named "Chapter 11 Multiple Regression Examples.R" in RStudio. Make sure that you have the correct directory path for loading the data. In other words, if "C:\MyFSRrFiles" is not where you have your data, change this part of the script file so that the data load into RStudio. Once you have done this, run the code to produce the output shown in Figure 11.1. Copy and paste this figure into your word processing document.

2. Estimate the two multiple regression models described in this chapter with the same specification but where the sample is divided according to whether the observation occurred before or after 2000. Put these results into a table in your word processing document and write about what you have found.

3. Estimate a multiple regression model with standardized coefficients. Put your results into a table in your word processing document and write about what you have found.

4. Open the script file named "Chapter 11 Dummy Dependent Variable Examples.R" in RStudio. Make sure that you have the correct directory path for loading the data. In other words, if "C:\MyFSRrFiles" is not where you have your data, change this part of the script file so that the data load into RStudio. Once you have done this, run the code to produce the results presented in Table 11.11 of *FSR*. Copy and paste this figure into your word processing document.

5. Using the code at the bottom of "Chapter 11 Dummy Dependent Variable Examples.R" create a classification table for the BNL and the BNP models. Copy and paste this into your word processing document.

6. Calculate the proportionate reduction in error from a naive model to the BNL and from a naive model to the BNP. Write briefly about what you have learned from doing this.

Putting It All Together to Produce Effective Research

OVERVIEW

In Chapter 12 of *FSR*, we tie the broad lessons of the book together in order to help you on your way to producing compelling research. In the last chapter of this companion book, we have some exercises for you to get you moving in this direction.

EXERCISES

1. Launch RStudio and load the "GSS2016_Sample_Chap12.RData" data set. Once you have done this, you'll see that there are five variables in this subsample from the 2016 GSS: YEAR (2016 only), EDUC (highest year of schooling completed), SEX (male or female), RINCOM16 (respondent's income in 2016), and RACE (non-Hispanic whites and non-Hispanics blacks only). RINCOM16 will be the dependent variable in the exercises for this chapter. Run the commands necessary to output appropriate descriptive statistics for the dependent variable (including a box–whisker plot) and write a brief summary of what you have found. Copy and paste the box–whisker plot into your word processing document.

2. Estimate a two-variable regression model with RINCOM16 as the dependent variable and EDUC as the independent variable. Write about what you have found. Copy and paste the output into your word processing document.

3. Estimate a multiple regression model with EDUC, SEX (coded 1 for females and 0 for males), and RACE (coded 1 for non-Hispanic blacks and 0 for non-Hispanic whites) as independent variables, and RINCOM16 as the dependent variable. Put your results into a table in your word processing document and write about what you have found.

4. Estimate the same multiple regression model as above but reverse the coding of both dummy variables so that males are coded 1 and females are coded 0, and non-Hispanic whites are coded 1 and non-Hispanic blacks are coded 0. Put

these results into a table in your word processing document and write about what you have found.

5. Estimate a multiple regression model with standardized coefficients with EDUC and the dummy variables for SEX and RACE as the independent variables, and RINCOM16 as the dependent variable. Put your results into a table in your word processing document and write about what you have found.

6. Create an interaction term between the dummy variables that you created for female and non-Hispanic black respondents. Then estimate a multiple regression model with education, the dummy variables for females and non-Hispanic blacks, and the interaction term as the independent variables, and RINCOM16 as the dependent variable. Write a brief summary of what these results tell you.

References

Bansak, Kirk, Jens Hainmueller, and Dominik Hangartner. 2016. "How Economic, Humanitarian, and Religious Concerns Shape European Attitudes Toward Asylum Seekers." *Science* 354(6309):217–222.

Branton, Regina P., and Bradford S. Jones. 2005. "Reexamining Racial Attitudes: The Conditional Relationship Between Diversity and Socioeconomic Environment." *American Journal of Political Science* 49(2):359–372.

Esses, Victoria M., John F. Dovidio, Lynne M. Jackson, and Tamara L. Armstrong. 2001. "The Immigration Dilemma: The Role of Perceived Group Competition, Ethnic Prejudice, and National Identity." *Journal of Social Issues* 57(3):389–412.

King, Gary, Benjamin Schneer, and Ariel White. 2017. "How the News Media Activate Public Expression and Influence National Agendas." *Science* 358(6364): 776–780.

McLaren, Lauren M. 2003. "Anti-immigrant Prejudice in Europe: Contact, Threat Perception, and Preferences for the Exclusion of Migrants." *Social Forces* 81(3):909–936.

Perry, Samuel L., Ryon J. Cobb, Andrew L. Whitehead, and Joshua B. Grubbs. 2021. "Divided by Faith (in Christian America): Christian Nationalism, Race, and Divergent Perceptions of Racial Injustice." *Social Forces*, soab134, https://doi.org/10.1093/sf/soab134.

Scarborough, William J., Joanna R. Pepin, Danny L. Lambouths III, Ronald Kwon, and Ronaldo Monasterio. 2021. "The Intersection of Racial and Gender Attitudes, 1977 Through 2018." *American Sociological Review* 86(5):823–855.

Sullivan, Jas M., and Alexandra Ghara. 2015. "Racial Identity and Intergroup Attitudes: A Multiracial Youth Analysis." *Social Science Quarterly* 96(1):261–272.

Index